THE

"I LOVE MY NUTRI BULLET"

GREEN SMOOTHIES

RECIPE BOOK

200 GREEN SMOOTHIES
for Increased Energy,
Glowing Skin,
Weight Loss,
and More

AVON, MASSACHUSETTS

Published by
Adams Media, a division of F+W Media, Inc.
57 Littlefield Street, Avon, MA 02322. U.S.A.
www.adamsmedia.com

Contains material adapted from *The Everything® Green Smoothies Book* by Britt Brandon, copyright © 2011 by F+W Media, Inc., ISBN 10: 1-4405-2564-1, ISBN 13: 978-1-4405-2564-3; *Paleo Green Smoothies* by Michelle Fagone, copyright © 2016 by F+W Media, Inc., ISBN 10: 1-4405-9293-4, ISBN 13: 978-1-4405-9293-5; *The Everything® Healthy Green Drinks Book* by Britt Brandon, copyright © 2014 by F+W Media, Inc., ISBN 10: 1-4405-7694-7, ISBN 13: 978-1-4405-7694-2; *The "I Love My NutriBullet" Recipe Book* by Britt Brandon, copyright © 2015 by F+W Media, Inc., ISBN 10: 1-4405-9208-X, ISBN 13: 978-1-4405-9208-9.

ISBN 10: 1-4405-9842-8
ISBN 13: 978-1-4405-9842-5
eISBN 10: 1-4405-9843-6
eISBN 13: 978-1-4405-9843-2

Printed in the United States of America.

10   9   8   7   6   5   4   3   2   1

The information in this book should not be used for diagnosing or treating any health problem. Not all diet and exercise plans suit everyone. You should always consult a trained medical professional before starting a diet, taking any form of medication, or embarking on any fitness or weight-training program. The author and publisher disclaim any liability arising directly or indirectly from the use of this book.

Always follow safety and commonsense cooking protocol while using kitchen utensils, operating ovens and stoves, and handling uncooked food. If children are assisting in the preparation of any recipe, they should always be supervised by an adult.

Many of the designations used by manufacturers and sellers to distinguish their products are claimed as trademarks. Where those designations appear in this book and F+W Media, Inc. was aware of a trademark claim, the designations have been printed with initial capital letters.

This book is unofficial and unauthorized. It is not authorized, approved, licensed, or endorsed by NutriBullet, LLC. NutriBullet is a registered trademark of Homeland Housewares, LLC.

Cover design by Sylvia McArdle.
Cover images © iStockphoto.com/aluxum; kaspri/123RF.

This book is available at quantity discounts for bulk purchases.
For information, please call 1-800-289-0963.

CONTENTS

CHAPTER 5   Smoothies for Better Digestive Health / 80

CHAPTER 6   Smoothies for Antiaging, Better Skin, and Body Care / 109

INTRODUCTION

Green smoothies that boost your energy.
Green smoothies that cleanse and detox.
Green smoothies that give you better skin and a thinner, healthier body.

Throughout this book you'll find 200 recipes that provide all of these health benefits and more! And, best of all, each of these green smoothies—smoothies that contain a mixture of greens and fruit—are made even more beneficial by being mixed in the NutriBullet.

The NutriBullet is not quite a blender and it's not quite a juicer. Instead, it's a device that combines the best features of both to offer you a path to healthy living. By using it, you can create smoothies that contain both juice and fiber (unlike those created by most juicers, which tend to remove the fiber), which is especially important when you're trying to reap the multitude of nutritional benefits found in green smoothies. Greens like lettuce, spinach, watercress, celery, and more can be difficult to digest. But the NutriBullet's innovative extractor blade releases the fiber, vitamins, minerals, antioxidants, oils, and enzymes from within every cell of these greens—unleashing powerful, potent nutritional benefits that are then available for immediate use throughout the body.

And making these nutrient-packed green smoothies in the NutriBullet is incredibly easy. Just put some fruits and vegetables in bags beforehand in premeasured amounts. Then pull them out of the fridge, put them in the NutriBullet's 24-ounce cup (being careful not to overload), and enjoy a healthy, wholesome smoothie that is yours to drink immediately or take on the go. You'll also find designations for each recipe throughout the book and in an appendix that tell you if a smoothie is vegan, paleo, sweet, or savory to help you plan your time in advance. In addition, the equipment is simple to maintain (cleaning takes around a minute), and it's relatively inexpensive.

So whether your goal is to get healthy, stay healthy, or improve a specific area of your health, the results you seek are well within reach. Just grab your NutriBullet and begin enjoying all of the delicious benefits of green smoothies today.

CHAPTER 1

GREEN SMOOTHIES: GOOD FOR YOU AND YOUR NUTRIBULLET

Most people know that greens are very nutritious but struggle to eat enough of them—they're not the easiest vegetables to prepare tastefully while maintaining all of the important vitamins and minerals your body requires. Steaming, sautéing, baking, and roasting vegetables cause them to lose the vitamins and minerals you're trying to consume by eating them in the first place. Greens can also be hard to digest—you may not get the full benefits from your average meal or salad containing greens because the greens themselves can be difficult to digest and tedious to chew to the point where digestion would be easy.

Fortunately, the NutriBullet's extractor blade breaks through the cell membranes that trap the carbohydrates, proteins, fats, vitamins, and minerals your body needs to thrive, and its exclusive cyclonic action liquefies the ingredients, providing easily absorbable nourishment to your digestive system, bloodstream, and entire body. Every sip of each NutriBullet-mixed green smoothie contains fiber, vitamins, minerals, and phytochemicals that would otherwise pass right through your body, costing you much of the nutrition content.

But what ingredients—green and otherwise—should you have on hand to include in your green "NutriBlast" smoothie? Read on . . .

LEAFY GREENS

Your green smoothie isn't complete without a dose of vibrant leafy greens. Research shows that leafy greens are one of the most concentrated sources of nutrition. They supply iron, calcium, potassium, magnesium, folate, and vitamins K, C, E, B_6, and B_{12} in abundance. Leafy greens also provide a variety of phytonutrients, including beta carotene and lutein, which protect cells from damage and eyes from age-related problems. A few cups of leafy greens also contain small amounts of omega-3 fatty acids and nine times the RDA for vitamin K, which regulates blood clotting, protects bones from osteoporosis, and may reduce the risk of atherosclerosis by reducing calcium in arterial plaques.

Here are some of the most popular leafy greens used for smoothies:

- **Lettuce.** Deep green lettuce is a good source of calcium, chlorophyll, iron, magnesium, potassium, silicon, and vitamins A and E. All types help rebuild hemoglobin, add shine and thickness to hair, and promote hair growth. Iceberg contains natural opiates that relax the muscles and nerves. Lettuce works best in combination with other vegetables. Wash carefully, refrigerate, and use within a few days.
- **Parsley.** Packed with chlorophyll, vitamins A and C, calcium, magnesium, phosphorous, potassium, sodium, and sulfur, parsley helps stimulate oxygen metabolism, cell respiration, and regeneration. Wash, refrigerate, and use within five days.
- **Spinach, kale, and Swiss chard.** Popeye was right all along: You'll be strong to the finish if you eat your spinach, kale, and chard, which are similar in nutritional value and provide ample supplies of iron, phosphorous, fiber, and vitamins A, B, C, E, and K. Wash thoroughly and bag loosely in the refrigerator. Use within four days.
- **Watercress.** This delicate, leafy green veggie has a slightly pungent taste and is packed with vitamin C, calcium, and potassium. It also contains acid-forming minerals, which make it ideal for intestinal cleansing and normalizing, and chlorophyll, which stimulates metabolism and circulatory functions. Refrigerate and use within five days.
- **Wheatgrass.** The juice from wheat berries contains many antiaging properties, including chlorophyll, a full spectrum of minerals, various enzymes, and vitamins A, B complex, and E. Refrigerate and use within four days.

CRUCIFEROUS VEGGIES

From broccoli and cauliflower to Brussels sprouts, kale, cabbage, and bok choy, the members of the cruciferous, or cabbage, family pack a nutritional wallop. They contain phytochemicals, vitamins, minerals, and fiber that are important to your health. Studies show that sulforaphane—one of the phytochemicals found in cruciferous vegetables—stimulates enzymes in the body that detoxify carcinogens before they damage cells.

Here's a rundown of the most delicious and nutritious root crops:

- **Broccoli.** Packed with fiber to help regularity, broccoli is also surprisingly high in protein, and it's packed with calcium, antioxidants, and vitamins B_6, C, and E. Because of its strong flavor, broccoli works best combined with other vegetables in juices rather than juiced alone. Wash well and use within four days to get maximum nutrients.
- **Cabbage.** Another member of the fiber-filled cruciferous family, cabbage comes in many different varieties, from white cabbage, which also comes in red and green, to savoy cabbage, with delicate, crinkly leaves. Other members of the cabbage family you can use in your smoothies include kale, collard greens, Brussels sprouts, and Chinese (napa) cabbage. All have large stores of vitamins B_6 and C. Kale and collard greens also have a lot of vitamin A and calcium. Members of the cabbage family are also packed with minerals.
- **Cauliflower.** Like other cruciferous vegetables, because of its strong flavor, cauliflower works best as a contributing player rather than a solo act. High in vitamin C and fiber, it has a more delicate taste than other cruciferous veggies. Use within four days or refrigerate for up to a week.

ROOT VEGETABLES

Classified by their fleshy underground storage unit, or root, which is a holding tank of nutrients, root vegetables are low in fat and high in natural sugars and fiber. Root veggies are also the perfect foods to eat when you need sustained energy and focus.

Some of the most nutritious root veggies include those with orangey skins, including carrots, squash, and sweet potatoes. The orange skin signifies they contain beta carotene, a powerful antioxidant that fights damaging free radicals.

Here are some delicious and nutritious root vegetables to include in your smoothies:

- **Beet and beet greens.** Both the beet greens and beetroots are blendable and highly nutritious. The roots are packed with calcium, potassium, and vitamins A and C. Choose small to medium beets with fresh green leaves and roots. Use greens within two days and beets within two weeks.
- **Carrot.** Carrots lend a mild, sweet taste to smoothies and taste equally delicious on their own. Carrots are packed with vitamins A, B, C, D, E, and K, as well as calcium, phosphorous, potassium, sodium, and trace minerals. Carrots stimulate digestion; improve hair, skin, and nails; have a mild diuretic effect; and cleanse the liver, helping to release bile and excess fats. Remove foliage when you get home, because it drains moisture and nutrients from the carrots. Refrigerate and use within a week.
- **Celery.** High in vitamin C and potassium with natural sodium, celery has a mild flavor that blends well with other veggies. Its natural sodium balances the pH of the blood and helps the body use calcium better. Choose firm, bright-green stalks with fresh green leaves. Refrigerate for up to a week.
- **Fennel.** Similar to celery in nutrients and high in sodium, calcium, and magnesium, fennel has a licorice-like taste that enhances the taste of juices made from vegetables with a strong flavor. Choose fennel bulbs the size of tennis balls with no bruising or discoloration. Refrigerate and use within five days.
- **Garlic.** A member of the lily family, this aromatic bulb, high in antioxidants for reducing cholesterol and heart disease, adds flavor and tang. Use one or two cloves per quart. Choose firm, smooth heads and store in a cool, dry place. Use within two weeks.
- **Ginger.** Technically a rhizome and native to Asia, ginger has a sweet, peppery flavor that enhances juice. Buy large, firm nodules with shiny skin. Refrigerate and use within a week.
- **Green onion.** Green onions are high in disease-fighting antioxidants and have the mildest flavor of the onion family, making them ideal for blending. They also have antibacterial properties that fight infections and skin diseases. Green onions should be firm and deep green in color. Refrigerate and use within a week.

- **Parsnip.** Cousins to the carrot, parsnips are packed with vitamin C, potassium, silicon, and phosphorous. Choose large, firm parsnips with feathery foliage. Refrigerate and use within a week.
- **Potato.** High in vitamins C and B and potassium, potatoes add a light flavor to smoothies. Store in a cool, dry place and use within two weeks.
- **Radish.** Small but mighty in taste and loaded with vitamin C, iron, magnesium, and potassium, radish juice cleanses the nasal sinuses and gastrointestinal tract and helps clear up skin disorders. Use a handful to add zing. Refrigerate and use within a week.
- **Turnip and turnip greens.** Ounce for ounce, turnip greens have more calcium than milk. The root supplies calcium, potassium, and magnesium. Together, they neutralize overly acidic blood and strengthen bones, hair, nails, and teeth. Store turnips at room temperature, scrub well, and use within two weeks. Refrigerate greens and use within a week.
- **Sweet potato and yam.** High in beta carotene, vitamin C, calcium, and potassium, these two vegetables have a similar taste and can be substituted for one another in recipes. Store in a cool, dry place.

VEGGIES FROM THE VINE

From acorn squash to zucchini, vegetables straight from the vine deliver a cornucopia of nutrients and fiber. Vine vegetables are also especially easy to grow in small, compact gardens or in containers on patios.

- **Bell pepper.** High in vitamin C, red peppers are also high in vitamin A and are much sweeter than the green variety. Peppers contribute to beautiful skin and hair, while red peppers stimulate circulation and tone and cleanse the arteries and heart muscle. Store at room temperature. Before blending, wash gently with a mild Castile soap, pull out the large clump of seeds, and remove the cap.
- **Cucumber.** With their mild flavor, cukes complement other vegetables and go well with herbs. Cucumbers are high in vitamin A and silica, which help repair connective tissue and skin. Buy firm, dark-green cucumbers with a slightly bumpy skin. Use within four days.
- **String bean.** High in vitamin B, calcium, magnesium, potassium, protein, and sulfur, string beans are good for your overall metabolism as well as your hair, skin, and nails. They have a strong flavor and taste best when combined with other vegetables.

- **Summer squash and zucchini.** Rich in vitamin C, B vitamins, calcium, and potassium, summer squash has a bland flavor that works best with other vegetables. It helps cleanse and soothe the bladder and kidneys. Store in a cool, dry place. Use within a few weeks.
- **Tomato.** Tomatoes are a good source of lycopene, which has been proven to have anticancer properties, and vitamin C and potassium, which cleanse the liver and add to the body's store of minerals, especially calcium. Fresh tomato juice also stimulates circulation. Store at room temperature.

BERRIES

Red, blue, purple, or black—no matter what the color or size, berries are wonder foods that are loaded with phytochemicals, antioxidants, and other vitamins and minerals that help prevent cancer and many other diseases. Cranberries and blueberries also contain a substance that may prevent bladder infections.

- **Blueberry and blackberry.** Both berries are packed with saponins, which improve heart health, as well as disease-fighting antioxidants, vitamin C, minerals, and phytochemicals.
- **Cranberry.** High in vitamins A and C as well as B complex vitamins, cranberries help prevent bladder infections by keeping bacteria from clinging to the wall of the bladder. Cranberries help reduce asthma symptoms, diarrhea, fever, fluid retention, and skin disorders, as well as disorders of the kidney, urinary tract, and lungs. Cranberries also facilitate weight loss.
- **Raspberry.** Raspberries are packed with vitamin C and potassium and provide 64 calories per cup.
- **Strawberry.** Strawberries are packed with vitamin C, iron, calcium, magnesium, folate, and potassium—essential for immune-system function and for strong connective tissue. Strawberries also provide just 53 calories a cup.

TREE AND VINE FRUITS

From apples to watermelon, fruits of the tree and vine provide an abundance of life-enhancing and disease-fighting vitamins, minerals, antioxidants, and phytochemicals. Here are some of the most popular fruits:

- **Apple.** Rich in vitamins A and C; the B vitamins B_1 (thiamine), B_2 (riboflavin), B_6, B_7 (biotin), and B_9 (folic acid); and a host of minerals that promote healthy skin, hair, and nails, apples also contain pectin, a fiber that absorbs toxins, stimulates digestion, and helps reduce cholesterol. Apples are extremely versatile and blend well with other juices.
- **Apricot.** Apricots are high in beta carotene and vitamin A and are a good source of fiber and potassium.
- **Cherry.** Rich in vitamins A, B, and C, as well as minerals, cherries are potent alkalizers that reduce the acidity of the blood, making them effective in reducing gout, arthritis, and prostate disorders.
- **Grape.** High in caffeic acid, which helps fight cancer, grapes are also packed with bioflavonoids, which help the body absorb vitamin C. Grapes also contain resveratrol, a nutrient that helps prevent liver, lung, breast, and prostate cancer, and saponins, a nutrient that binds with cholesterol and prevents the body from absorbing it.
- **Grapefruit.** Rich in vitamin C, calcium, phosphorous, and potassium, the pink and red varieties of grapefruit are sweeter and less acidic than white grapefruit. Grapefruit helps strengthen capillary walls, heal bruising, and reduce skin infections, ear disorders, fever, indigestion, scurvy, varicose veins, obesity, and morning sickness.
- **Lemon.** Lemons are high in citric acid and vitamin C, so a little goes a long way in juicing. Their high antioxidant content and antibacterial properties relieve colds, sore throats, and skin infections and also help reduce anemia, blood disorders, constipation, ear disorders, gout, indigestion, scurvy, skin infections, and obesity.
- **Lime.** Similar to lemons in nutrients but not as acidic or cleansing, limes can be substituted for lemons in juice recipes.
- **Orange.** A rich source of vitamins C, B (biotin, folic acid), and K, plus amino acids and minerals, oranges cleanse the gastrointestinal tract, strengthen capillary walls, and benefit the heart and lungs. Oranges help reduce anemia, blood disorders, colds, fever, heart disease, high blood pressure, liver disorders, lung disorders, skin disorders, pneumonia, rheumatism, scurvy, and obesity.
- **Peach and nectarine.** High in beta carotene, vitamins B (niacin) and C, and minerals, peaches and nectarines cleanse the intestines and help relieve morning sickness.

- **Pear.** Rich in fiber and vitamins C and B (folic acid, niacin), and the minerals phosphorous and calcium, pears help reduce disorders of the bladder, liver, and prostate as well as constipation.
- **Plum.** High in vitamins C and A, copper, and iron, the benzoic and quinic acids in plums are effective laxatives. Plums help with anemia, constipation, and weight loss.

MELONS

Melons are the juiciest fruit by far, and naturals for fresh smoothies. They come in many varieties, including canary, cantaloupe, casaba, crenshaw, honeydew, and mush. They are sweet and fun summertime thirst quenchers. All varieties are rich in vitamins A, B complex, and C, and they promote skin and nerve health. Melons provide enzymes and natural unconcentrated sugars that help aid digestion. Here are some popular melons that you'll want to include in your green smoothies:

- **Cantaloupe.** High in beta carotene, vitamin C, and potassium, it alleviates disorders of the bladder, kidney, and skin and reduces constipation.
- **Honeydew.** High in potassium and vitamin C, and when blended into smoothies, it promotes energy. It alleviates disorders of the bladder, kidney, and skin and reduces constipation.
- **Watermelon.** High in electrolytes and rich in vitamin A and the mineral potassium, it quenches thirst and also helps cleanse the kidney and bladder. Watermelon helps reduce discomfort associated with aging, arthritis, bladder disorders, constipation, fluid retention, kidney disorders, pregnancy, prostate problems, and skin disorders, and it promotes weight loss.

TROPICAL FRUIT

You can find a bounty of tropical fruit in your local supermarket, even if you live in a cold climate, including:

- **Avocado.** Although frequently mistaken for a vegetable, the avocado is actually a member of the pear family. Avocados are rich in vitamins A, C, and E. Ripe avocados can be refrigerated for up to five days.

- **Banana.** Bananas are a great source of potassium, an essential electrolyte, as well as magnesium and vitamin B_6.
- **Kiwifruit.** Kiwis are rich in vitamins A and C and contain nearly as much potassium as bananas. Their fuzzy skins contain valuable antioxidants and can also be used in marinades for tenderizing meats.
- **Mango.** Like other orange-colored produce, mangos are packed with beta carotene.
- **Papaya.** Papayas are loaded with papain, an enzyme that promotes digestion and has been shown to protect the stomach from ulcers. Papayas are also rich in vitamins A and C, and have an abundance of natural sugars. Papayas can also help reduce acidosis, acne, heart disease, tumors, ulcers, and blood disorders.
- **Pineapple.** A great source of potassium, calcium, iron, and iodine, fresh pineapple is worth the hassle required to prepare it for smoothies. Using a strong knife, slice off the top and bottom of the pineapple so it sits flat on your cutting board, and then slice off the peel.

TEAS

Brewed, cooled teas, caffeinated or not, green or black or otherwise, can add depth of flavor to your green smoothies. Teas are also known to have a variety of medicinal and pampering effects. Substitute cooled teas for water in any of your smoothies. You can also freeze some in ice cube trays. This will allow you to add them to your smoothies without watering down the drink.

So now that you know what to have on hand to create nutritious, green NutriBlast smoothies, let's take a look at the delicious recipes and see what they have to offer. Enjoy!

CHAPTER 2

SMOOTHIES FOR BETTER IMMUNITY

With super smoothie recipes that combine ingredients designed to improve your health with great taste in every sip, the NutriBullet can help improve your immune system and fend off illness. Citrus fruits, vibrant greens, and ginger are just a few of the players featured in these immunity-boosting super smoothies. Sweet or savory, the flavors that combine to create delicious, any-time-of-day smoothies like the Cucumber Zing, Herbal Peach, and Ginger and Spice Make Everything Nice will help you achieve the healthiness you deserve.

Powerful vitamins and minerals combine with phytochemicals in these green smoothies to combat illness and disease. At the same time, they protect the body's systems and cells from harmful changes that can result from oxidative stress, toxins, or prolonged inflammation. The super green smoothies in this section boast green fruits, vegetables, and additions that not only taste great when blended together but boost immune-system functioning to optimize health and minimize illnesses—mild, moderate, or severe!

CANTALOUPE QUENCHER

Vegan, Sweet, Paleo

Although many people get the flu shot, exercise regularly, and try to eat a diet that will promote illness protection, when was the last time you found yourself guzzling vitamin C for the health benefits or finishing off your spinach because of the rich iron content? You want to eat what tastes great, and when you make nutritious food delicious, you can arm your body with the immunity-building protection packed into this delicious green smoothie.

24 OUNCES

1 cup shredded iceberg lettuce

2 cups peeled and seeded cantaloupe

2 small bananas, peeled and sliced

¾ cup unsweetened almond milk

1 cup ice

1. Combine lettuce, cantaloupe, bananas, and ¾ cup almond milk in the 24-ounce NutriBullet cup and blend until thoroughly combined.

2. Add ice and blend until smooth.

3. Consume immediately or store with an airtight lid in the refrigerator for no more than 3–4 hours.

PER 24-OUNCE SERVING		
CALORIES: 319	FAT: 2.8 G	PROTEIN: 6.3 G
SODIUM: 180 MG	FIBER: 9.0 G	
CARBOHYDRATES: 74.4 G		SUGAR: 51.3 G

ORANGE YOU GLAD YOU GOT UP FOR THIS?

Vegan, Sweet, Paleo

Packed with brain-stimulating and immune-protecting vitamin C, this smoothie is a great option when everyone around you seems to be sick. Its power is intensified with the antioxidant-rich CoconutMilk.

24 OUNCES

1 cup iceberg lettuce

3 small oranges, peeled and seeds removed

½ cup unsweetened CoconutMilk

1. Combine lettuce and oranges in the 24-ounce NutriBullet cup and blend until just combined.

2. Add CoconutMilk and blend until thoroughly combined.

3. Consume immediately or store with an airtight lid in the refrigerator for no more than 3–4 hours.

PER 24-OUNCE SERVING		
CALORIES: 164	FAT: 2.2 G	PROTEIN: 3.2 G
SODIUM: 22 MG	FIBER: 7.6 G	
CARBOHYDRATES: 35.5 G		SUGAR: 28.1 G

Vitamin C

Oranges are well-known for their immunity-building power, and rightfully so! By consuming oranges every day, the human body can fight off illnesses from the common cold to serious cancers and heart disease. You can thank the rich beta carotene and the vitamin C. An orange can definitely improve your health and longevity.

GINGER AND SPICE MAKE EVERYTHING NICE

Vegan, Sweet, Paleo

This smoothie is packed with the delicious sweet and spicy flavor of ginger. By including ginger with greens and banana, the phytochemicals and antioxidants in this smoothie are powerful in boosting immunity, deterring health risks, and improving the natural functions of body processes.

24 OUNCES

2"–3" knob ginger, peeled and sliced

¾ cup unsweetened almond milk

1 teaspoon ground cloves

1 cup baby greens

1 small banana, peeled and sliced

1. Combine the ginger slices and ¾ cup almond milk in the 24-ounce NutriBullet cup and blend until milk has thickened.

2. Once thickened, add the cloves, baby greens, and banana and blend until thoroughly combined.

3. Consume immediately or store with an airtight lid in the refrigerator for no more than 3–4 hours.

PER 24-OUNCE SERVING		
CALORIES: 121	FAT: 2.3 G	PROTEIN: 2.6 G
SODIUM: 158 MG	FIBER: 4.0 G	
CARBOHYDRATES: 27.1 G		SUGAR: 12.5 G

CUCUMBER ZING

Vegan, Sweet, Paleo

Cucumbers offer up a wide variety of important vitamins and minerals while lending a refreshing and hydrating background to the spicy ginger in this smoothie. This blend will whet your appetite while building your immunity!

24 OUNCES

1 cup watercress

2 small cucumbers, peeled and sliced

2 small oranges, peeled and seeds removed

¼" knob ginger, peeled

¾ cup water

1. Combine watercress, cucumbers, oranges, ginger, and ¾ cup water in the 24-ounce NutriBullet cup and blend until thoroughly combined.

2. Consume immediately or store with an airtight lid in the refrigerator for no more than 3–4 hours.

PER 24-OUNCE SERVING		
CALORIES: 130	FAT: 0.2 G	PROTEIN: 4.5 G
SODIUM: 26 MG	FIBER: 7.0 G	
CARBOHYDRATES: 29.9 G		SUGAR: 22.4 G

LUSCIOUS LEMON

Vegan, Savory, Paleo

Lemon makes for a refreshing ingredient packed with vitamin C. Not only does this vitamin aid in building immunity, but it plays an important role in the metabolism of fat!

24 OUNCES

1 cup watercress

2 small lemons, peeled and seeds removed

2 celery stalks

2 small cucumbers, peeled and sliced

½" knob ginger, peeled

1¾ cups water, divided

1. Combine watercress, lemons, celery, cucumbers, ginger, and 1 cup water in the 24-ounce NutriBullet cup and blend until thoroughly combined.

2. Add remaining ¾ cup water and blend until combined.

3. Consume immediately or store with an airtight lid in the refrigerator for no more than 3–4 hours.

PER 24-OUNCE SERVING		
CALORIES: 85	FAT: 0.3 G	PROTEIN: 4.5 G
SODIUM: 101 MG	FIBER: 6.9 G	
CARBOHYDRATES: 20.7 G		SUGAR: 8.4 G

Vegan, Sweet, Paleo

Protect your body from illness by packing in the vitamin C. Not only does this amazing vitamin promote health and immunity, but it can alleviate stress and improve mental stability and happiness.

24 OUNCES

1 cup watercress

2 small oranges, peeled and seeds removed

½ small pineapple, peeled, cored, and cubed

½ small lemon, peeled and seeds removed

½ small lime, peeled and seeds removed

½ cup cooled red raspberry tea

1. Combine watercress, oranges, pineapple, lemon, and lime in the 24-ounce NutriBullet cup and blend until thoroughly combined.

2. Add ½ cup tea and blend until combined.

3. Consume immediately or store with an airtight lid in the refrigerator for no more than 3–4 hours.

PER 24-OUNCE SERVING		
CALORIES: 255	FAT: 0.4 G	PROTEIN: 4.5 G
SODIUM: 18 MG	FIBER: 11.9 G	
CARBOHYDRATES: 69.0 G		SUGAR: 44.8 G

CITRUS BERRY BLAST

Vegan, Sweet, Paleo

There is nothing more refreshing and uplifting than sweet citrus! Mind in a fog? Stress levels high? Smoothie combinations like this immunity-boosting one are a delightful remedy to what ails the mind and body!

24 OUNCES

1 cup watercress

3 small oranges, peeled and seeds removed

½ small grapefruit, peeled and seeds removed

1 cup strawberries, tops removed

1 cup blueberries

1 cup water

1. Combine watercress, oranges, grapefruit, berries, and 1 cup water in the 24-ounce NutriBullet cup and blend until thoroughly combined.

2. Consume immediately or store with an airtight lid in the refrigerator for no more than 3–4 hours.

PER 24-OUNCE SERVING		
CALORIES: 332	FAT: 0.8 G	PROTEIN: 6.8 G
SODIUM: 24 MG	FIBER: 15.7 G	
CARBOHYDRATES: 82.9 G		SUGAR: 62.7 G

HERBAL PEACH

Vegan, Sweet, Paleo

Green tea is the ingredient responsible for loading antioxidants into this flavorful smoothie! It's easy to combat illnesses and promote health and wellness for your body and mind with this quick and easy recipe.

24 OUNCES

1 cup spinach

2 tablespoons chopped parsley

2 small peaches, pitted and peeled

½ small lemon, peeled and seeds removed

1½ cups cooled green tea

1. Combine spinach, parsley, peaches, lemon, and 1½ cups tea in the 24-ounce NutriBullet cup and blend until thoroughly combined.

2. Consume immediately or store with an airtight lid in the refrigerator for no more than 3–4 hours.

PER 24-OUNCE SERVING		
CALORIES: 120	FAT: 0.5 G	PROTEIN: 3.8 G
SODIUM: 30 MG	FIBER: 5.6 G	
CARBOHYDRATES: 29.8 G		SUGAR: 22.7 G

Green Tea's Power

The importance of green tea can be seen in its use in Eastern medicinal culture. Used as a remedy for many illnesses and to promote natural health, green tea's amazing health benefits come from its rich concentration of powerful antioxidants. Antioxidants combat serious illnesses and disease and cleanse the body of toxins and waste, all while providing improved immunity, optimal functioning of the body's processes, and a great-tasting substitute to water.

FRUITY FRESH IMMUNITY BLAST

Vegan, Sweet, Paleo

Cantaloupe and honeydew mix with spinach to make a sweet blend that's a delightful difference from the same old green smoothie. Providing rich antioxidants for health and immunity-building protection, this combo is a tasty way to deliver important nutrition to your body and keep yourself healthy.

24 OUNCES

1 cup spinach

1 cup peeled and seeded cantaloupe

1 cup honeydew, rind and seeds removed

1½ cups water

1. Combine spinach, cantaloupe, honeydew, and 1½ cups water in the 24-ounce NutriBullet cup and blend until thoroughly combined.

2. Consume immediately or store with an airtight lid in the refrigerator for no more than 3–4 hours.

PER 24–OUNCE SERVING		
CALORIES: 121	FAT: 0.4 G	PROTEIN: 3.1 G
SODIUM: 79 MG	FIBER: 3.5 G	
CARBOHYDRATES: 29.6 G		SUGAR: 26.5 G

Sweet

Grapefruit and cucumber combine in this smoothie to offer a refreshing zing to your morning. It provides lots of vitamins and nutrients that will wake you up and keep you feeling fresh throughout the day. Although grapefruit is known for being rich in vitamin C, this citrus fruit has been used for building immunity and for treating symptoms of illness such as common colds and bone disorders. The next time you start feeling feverish, the best thing to take may be a healthy helping of this grapefruit smoothie.

24 OUNCES

2 cups baby greens

2 small Bartlett pears, peeled, cored, and sliced

1 small cucumber, peeled and sliced

Juice from 2 small red grapefruits

¼ cup water

2 teaspoons raw honey

1. Combine greens, pears, cucumber, grapefruit juice, water, and honey in the 24-ounce NutriBullet cup and blend until thoroughly combined.

2. Consume immediately or store with an airtight lid in the refrigerator for no more than 3–4 hours.

PER 24-OUNCE SERVING		
CALORIES: 403	FAT: 1.1 G	PROTEIN: 5.1 G
SODIUM: 76 MG	FIBER: 11.5 G	
CARBOHYDRATES: 99.4 G		SUGAR: 43.0 G

CHAPTER 3

SMOOTHIES FOR WEIGHT LOSS

The NutriBullet green smoothies in this chapter—like the Minty Mango Metabolism Maximizer, the Savory Slim Down, and the Super Celery Smoothie—are a great way to get a satisfying meal substitute or snack when you're trying to shed a few pounds. Packed full of fiber, vitamin C, antioxidants, and more, the fruits, nuts, teas, and other ingredients all help boost your metabolism, suppress your appetite, flush out your system, and help you achieve or maintain weight loss. And these smoothies are prepared quickly enough to meet anyone's scheduling demands. Nutritious, fast, and easy, these NutriBullet green smoothies are sure to set you up for weight-loss success!

GREEN TEA METABOLISM BOOSTER

Vegan, Sweet, Paleo

Green tea is packed with fat-burning catechin antioxidants that aid in weight loss. Using green tea instead of water in this smoothie amplifies the fat-burning properties of the vitamin- and mineral-rich greens and fruits.

24 OUNCES

1 cup watercress

1 small lemon, peeled and seeds removed

2 cups peeled and seeded cantaloupe

1 cup raspberries

1¼ cups cooled green tea

1. Combine watercress, lemon, cantaloupe, raspberries, and 1¼ cups tea in the 24-ounce NutriBullet cup and blend until thoroughly combined.

2. Consume immediately or store with an airtight lid in the refrigerator for no more than 3–4 hours.

PER 24-OUNCE SERVING		
CALORIES: 192	FAT: 1.1 G	PROTEIN: 5.6 G
SODIUM: 68 MG	FIBER: 12.7 G	
CARBOHYDRATES: 47.3 G		SUGAR: 32.1 G

Making Quick Green Tea

Most people who are on the go prefer to make their green tea with the conveniently prepackaged tea bags. By purchasing quality green tea bags and using quality purified and filtered water, you can make your own fat-burning green tea on the go, at the office, or even in the car. Boil the water and pour it into a safe (preferably glass) container, steep the tea bag for the suggested amount of time to maximize antioxidant release, and taste and enjoy!

CANTALOUPE CREATION

Vegan, Sweet, Paleo

Cantaloupe is rich in vitamins and minerals important for weight loss and maximizing metabolic rates. A tasty treat for breakfast, lunch, or dinner, this satisfying combination of delightful flavors makes for a great fat-burning meal replacement.

24 OUNCES

1 cup watercress

½ small cantaloupe, peeled and seeds removed

1 cup peeled, cored, and cubed pineapple

1 small orange, peeled and seeds removed

½" knob ginger, peeled

1½ cups cooled green tea

1. Combine watercress, cantaloupe, pineapple, orange, ginger, and 1½ cups tea in the 24-ounce NutriBullet cup and blend until thoroughly combined.

2. Consume immediately or store with an airtight lid in the refrigerator for no more than 3–4 hours.

PER 24-OUNCE SERVING		
CALORIES: 170	FAT: 0.3 G	PROTEIN: 3.5 G
SODIUM: 34 MG	FIBER: 5.8 G	
CARBOHYDRATES: 43.3 G		SUGAR: 34.0 G

Cantaloupe for Regulating Metabolism

Anyone who struggles with weight loss and management knows the downfalls of a slow metabolism. Affected by sleep, stress, diet, and activity levels, metabolism can be increased not only through lifestyle but also the foods we choose. Cantaloupe and other fruits and vegetables high in vitamin C play an important role in regulating and optimizing metabolism, making weight loss and management more successful.

BEET THE BLOAT

Vegan, Sweet, Paleo

Beets are high in vitamins, minerals, and antioxidants that promote your body's ability to function optimally. By combining beets with apples, lemon, ginger, and green tea, you can fuel your body with the nutrients it needs while optimizing its fat-burning potential.

24 OUNCES

1 cup beet greens

1 small beet

3 small apples, peeled, cored, and sliced

½ small lemon, peeled and seeds removed

¼" knob ginger, peeled

1½ cups cooled green tea

1. Combine beet greens, beet, apples, lemon, ginger, and 1½ cups tea in the 24-ounce NutriBullet cup and blend until thoroughly combined.

2. Consume immediately or store with an airtight lid in the refrigerator for no more than 3–4 hours.

PER 24-OUNCE SERVING		
CALORIES: 244	FAT: 0.4 G	PROTEIN: 3.6 G
SODIUM: 151 MG	FIBER: 10.0 G	
CARBOHYDRATES: 63.6 G		SUGAR: 46.5 G

Vegan, Sweet, Paleo

This smoothie will satisfy any craving while delivering loads of vitamins and nutrients for optimizing your energy and stamina. It makes an amazing meal or snack that will energize your body and mind while keeping your diet on track.

24 OUNCES

1 cup spinach

2 small red apples, peeled, cored, and sliced

2 small Bartlett pears, peeled, cored, and sliced

½ small lemon, peeled and seeds removed

¼" knob ginger, peeled

1½ cups cooled green tea

1. Combine spinach, apples, pears, lemon, ginger, and tea in the 24-ounce NutriBullet cup and blend until thoroughly combined.

2. Consume immediately or store with an airtight lid in the refrigerator for no more than 3–4 hours.

PER 24–OUNCE SERVING		
CALORIES: 331	FAT: 1.0 G	PROTEIN: 3.1 G
SODIUM: 26 MG	FIBER: 14.3 G	
CARBOHYDRATES: 83.3 G		SUGAR: 57 G

Benefits of Natural Carbs

The calories in fruits and vegetables are used in digestion and by body processes that function to perform normal activity, so there is virtually no waste of calories and none to be stored as fat. In addition, the carbohydrates of fruits and vegetables turn to sugars more slowly than refined carbohydrates, allowing them to burn fat without fluctuating blood sugar levels.

Vegan, Sweet, Paleo

By adding this green smoothie to your diet, you can ensure you're providing your body with a variety of vitamins and minerals that it requires to run at its optimal level. The ingredients of this smoothie make a tasty treat for your eyes and your body.

24 OUNCES

1 cup beet greens

1 small beet

1 small carrot, peeled, sliced, and tops removed

1 small apple, peeled, cored, and sliced

1 small banana, peeled and sliced

1¾ cups cooled green tea

1. Combine beet greens, beet, carrot, apple, banana, and 1¾ cups tea in the 24-ounce NutriBullet cup and blend until thoroughly combined.

2. Consume immediately or store with an airtight lid in the refrigerator for no more than 3–4 hours.

PER 24-OUNCE SERVING		
CALORIES: 218	FAT: 0.5 G	PROTEIN: 4.1 G
SODIUM: 186 MG	FIBER: 9.4 G	
CARBOHYDRATES: 55.1 G		SUGAR: 33.8 G

CINCH POUNDS WITH CITRUS

Vegan, Sweet, Paleo

This sweet combination of greens and citrus makes for a refreshing snack for your body and mind. This smoothie stimulates your brain for improved mental clarity and focus, your body for more efficient metabolism, and your overall health with the abundance of vitamins and minerals.

24 OUNCES

1 cup watercress

1 small grapefruit, peeled and seeds removed

½ small pineapple, peeled, cored, and cubed

1 small orange, peeled and seeds removed

½ small lemon, peeled and seeds removed

½ small lime, peeled and seeds removed

1½ cups cooled green tea

1. Combine watercress, grapefruit, pineapple, orange, lemon, lime, and 1½ cup tea in the 24-ounce NutriBullet cup and blend until thoroughly combined.

2. Consume immediately or store with an airtight lid in the refrigerator for no more than 3–4 hours.

PER 24-OUNCE SERVING		
CALORIES: 320	FAT: 0.5 G	PROTEIN: 6.1 G
SODIUM: 18 MG	FIBER: 12.1 G	
CARBOHYDRATES: 83.5 G		SUGAR: 62.6 G

Vitamin C

Some restrictive diets can leave your body feeling fatigued and your mind fuzzy. With those side effects, no wonder so many people abandon their diet plans! With an increase in vitamin C in your daily diet, your body's metabolism of proteins, fats, and carbohydrates improves, making for wonderful effects in mental clarity, improved energy and stamina, and a better feeling of fullness from your foods. It also improves the body's ability to remove toxins and waste.

APPLE PIE FOR WEIGHT LOSS

Vegan, Sweet, Paleo

Even the most avid dieter who sticks to every aspect of a diet gets hit with cravings now and again. This smoothie will satisfy your taste buds' desire for delicious apple pie without the unhealthy sugars, carbs, and lack of nutrition of the traditional treat.

24 OUNCES

1 cup watercress

3 small Granny Smith apples, peeled, cored, and sliced

½ small lemon, peeled and seeds removed

1 teaspoon ground cloves

½" knob ginger, peeled

1½ cups cooled green tea

1. Combine watercress, apples, lemon, cloves, ginger, and tea in the 24-ounce NutriBullet cup and blend until thoroughly combined.

2. Consume immediately or store with an airtight lid in the refrigerator for no more than 3–4 hours.

PER 24-OUNCE SERVING		
CALORIES: 209	FAT: 0.5 G	PROTEIN: 2.3 G
SODIUM: 21 MG	FIBER: 6.7 G	
CARBOHYDRATES: 56.0 G		SUGAR: 40.9 G

A Smart Way to Satisfy Cravings

A smart suggestion for diet success is to consume water or healthy fruits and vegetables when cravings strike! Green smoothies are an excellent option because they provide a large dose of greens, fruits, and vegetables tailored to fit your craving. Sweet smoothies can provide the sugar you're craving, and the savory options work wonders in calming your want for salt.

SMOOTH CARROT APPLE

Vegan, Sweet, Paleo

The delightfully sweet taste combination of carrots and apples downplays the spinach. Intensifying the effects of weight loss, the lemon and green tea act to fuel your body's fat-burning furnace for more efficient fat-burning ability!

24 OUNCES

1 cup spinach

3 small carrots, peeled, sliced, and tops removed

2 small apples, peeled, cored, and sliced

1 small banana, peeled and sliced

½ small lemon, peeled and seeds removed

1½ cups cooled green tea

1. Combine spinach, carrots, apples, banana, lemon, and 1½ cups tea in the 24-ounce NutriBullet cup and blend until thoroughly combined.

2. Consume immediately or store with an airtight lid in the refrigerator for no more than 3–4 hours.

PER 24-OUNCE SERVING		
CALORIES: 293	FAT: 0.7 G	PROTEIN: 4.4 G
SODIUM: 130 MG	FIBER: 11.7 G	
CARBOHYDRATES: 75.7 G		SUGAR: 47.0 G

SWEET GINGER MELON

Vegan, Sweet, Paleo

Cantaloupe and watermelon make for a hydrating pair in this green smoothie. Refreshing your body while providing loads of vitamins and minerals, these super fruits lend important water content, a must-have for successful diets.

24 OUNCES

1 cup watercress

½ small cantaloupe, peeled and seeds removed

1 cup cubed and seeded watermelon

½" knob ginger, peeled

1 cup cooled green tea

1. Combine watercress, cantaloupe, watermelon, ginger, and 1 cup tea in the 24-ounce NutriBullet cup and blend until thoroughly combined.

2. Consume immediately or store with an airtight lid in the refrigerator for no more than 3–4 hours.

PER 24-OUNCE SERVING		
CALORIES: 88	FAT: 0.3 G	PROTEIN: 2.7 G
SODIUM: 34 MG	FIBER: 1.8 G	
CARBOHYDRATES: 21.9 G		SUGAR: 18.2 G

The Importance of Water in Dieting

Hunger, fatigue, and lack of focus can all be terrible side effects of not providing your body with adequate water. Especially in restrictive diets that provide little water from foods, the importance of consuming adequate water is tenfold! If the blandness of water makes consuming the recommended amount unbearable, opt for green tea. If you prefer fruit juices, green smoothies with loads of fruits make a healthier option with far less sugar, preservatives, and additives.

GORGEOUS GREENS FOR A GORGEOUS BODY

Vegan, Sweet, Paleo

These gorgeous green fruits and veggies make a deliciously refreshing treat. Not only is this a filling smoothie option; the ingredients also offer up balanced nutrition, vitamins, minerals, and strong antioxidants that will keep you moving throughout your day.

24 OUNCES

1 cup spinach

2 small Granny Smith apples, peeled, cored, and sliced

2 celery stalks

1 small cucumber, peeled and sliced

½ small lime, peeled and seeds removed

1½ cups cooled green tea

1. Combine spinach, apples, celery, cucumber, lime, and 1½ cups tea in the 24-ounce NutriBullet cup and blend until thoroughly combined.

2. Consume immediately or store with an airtight lid in the refrigerator for no more than 3–4 hours.

PER 24-OUNCE SERVING		
CALORIES: 175	FAT: 0.4 G	PROTEIN: 3.3 G
SODIUM: 93 MG	FIBER: 7.4 G	
CARBOHYDRATES: 44.9 G		SUGAR: 30.6 G

Total Health Inside and Out

The natural nutrition found in greens and fruits can do wonders for your body on the inside and out! Consuming deep greens and vibrant fruits and veggies, hydrating with water, and exercising daily combine for health benefits you can see and feel. Improved energy to help you run faster and farther, mental clarity to keep you focused on your goals and how to accomplish them, faster metabolism, improved recovery time, and beautiful skin, hair, and nails are all added benefits of sound nutrition.

ASPARAGUS CARROT

Vegan, Savory, Paleo

Asparagus is a well-known diuretic that works wonders on those days when the scale says one thing and your jeans say another. A great light meal or satisfying snack, this smoothie will fill you up without weighing you down!

24 OUNCES

1 cup watercress

1 cup chopped asparagus

3 small carrots, peeled, sliced, and tops removed

1 celery stalk

1 small garlic clove

1½ cups water

1. Combine watercress, asparagus, carrots, celery, garlic, and 1½ cups water in the 24-ounce NutriBullet cup and blend until thoroughly combined.

2. Consume immediately or store with an airtight lid in the refrigerator for no more than 3–4 hours.

PER 24-OUNCE SERVING		
CALORIES: 100	FAT: 0.4 G	PROTEIN: 5.6 G
SODIUM: 164 MG	FIBER: 7.9 G	
CARBOHYDRATES: 22.2 G		SUGAR: 10.3 G

A SPICY BLUE BLAST

Vegan, Sweet, Paleo

Antioxidant-rich blueberries and fat-burning blackberries pair up with soothing ginger for a refreshingly light smoothie that will make any diet more enjoyable! These sweet ingredients can even be enjoyed as a midnight snack without the guilt of the alternatives.

24 OUNCES

1 cup watercress

2 cups blueberries

1 cup blackberries

½" knob ginger, peeled

1¼ cups cooled green tea

1. Combine watercress, berries, ginger, and 1¼ cups tea in the 24-ounce NutriBullet cup and blend until thoroughly combined.

2. Consume immediately or store with an airtight lid in the refrigerator for no more than 3–4 hours.

PER 24-OUNCE SERVING		
CALORIES: 234	FAT: 1.1 G	PROTEIN: 5.0 G
SODIUM: 18 MG	FIBER: 14.9 G	
CARBOHYDRATES: 58.0 G		SUGAR: 36.6 G

GINGER GREEN TEA SMOOTHIE

Vegan, Sweet, Paleo

Strawberries are superfoods disguised as sweet treats. These fat-burning fruits are low in calories, packed with antioxidants that promote weight loss, and supply quick energy that also allows you to burn fat fast. They are also rich in magnesium, one of the most important minerals when dieting, key to promoting energy regulation.

24 OUNCES

1 cup watercress

1 cup strawberries, tops removed

2 small apples, peeled, cored and sliced

½" knob ginger, peeled

1½ cups cooled green tea

1. Combine watercress, strawberries, apples, ginger, and 1½ cups tea in the 24-ounce NutriBullet cup and blend until thoroughly combined.

2. Consume immediately or store with an airtight lid in the refrigerator for no more than 3–4 hours.

PER 24-OUNCE SERVING		
CALORIES: 178	FAT: 0.5 G	PROTEIN: 2.5 G
SODIUM: 17 MG	FIBER: 6.5 G	
CARBOHYDRATES: 46.1 G		SUGAR: 33.8 G

Vegan, Savory, Paleo

With the savory smoothie options available, your desire for salty unhealthy alternatives can be satisfied healthfully. Enjoy this vitamin- and mineral-packed recipe for a savory and satisfying meal option that will deliver sound nutrition, great taste, and zero guilt.

24 OUNCES

1 cup spinach

1 cup chopped asparagus

1 small tomato, sliced

1 small green onion, trimmed and chopped

1 small garlic clove

1½ cups water, divided

1. Combine spinach, asparagus, tomato, onion, garlic, and ¾ cup water in the 24-ounce NutriBullet cup and blend until thoroughly combined.

2. Add remaining ¾ cup water and blend until combined.

3. Consume immediately or store with an airtight lid in the refrigerator for no more than 3–4 hours.

PER 24-OUNCE SERVING		
CALORIES: 72	FAT: 1.2 G	PROTEIN: 5.1 G
SODIUM: 44 MG	FIBER: 4.7 G	
CARBOHYDRATES: 14.7 G		SUGAR: 8.8 G

GARLIC GETS THE POUNDS OFF

Vegan, Savory, Paleo

In addition to delivering strong vitamins and minerals, excellent antioxidants, and an amazing amount of health benefits for your heart, garlic provides an astounding amount of protection against illness.

24 OUNCES

1 cup romaine lettuce

1 cup broccoli spears

1 celery stalk

1 small tomato, sliced

1 small green onion, trimmed and chopped

2 small garlic cloves

2 cups water, divided

1. Combine romaine, broccoli, celery, tomato, onion, garlic, and 1 cup water in the 24-ounce NutriBullet cup and blend until thoroughly combined.

2. Add remaining 1 cup water and blend until combined.

3. Consume immediately or store with an airtight lid in the refrigerator for no more than 3–4 hours.

PER 24–OUNCE SERVING		
CALORIES: 68	FAT: 0.4 G	PROTEIN: 4.7 G
SODIUM: 88 MG	FIBER: 5.3 G	
CARBOHYDRATES: 14.7 G		SUGAR: 5.2 G

MINTY MANGO METABOLISM MAXIMIZER

Vegan, Sweet, Paleo

The delightful flavors of watercress, mango, oranges, and green tea are intensified by the addition of mint in this recipe. This refreshing smoothie is sweet—but not too sweet.

24 OUNCES

1 cup watercress

1 cup peeled, pitted, and cubed mango

2 small oranges, peeled and seeds removed

¼ cup mint leaves

1 cup cooled green tea, divided

1. Combine watercress, mango, oranges, mint, and ½ cup tea in the 24-ounce NutriBullet cup and blend until thoroughly combined.

2. Add remaining ½ cup tea and blend until combined.

3. Consume immediately or store with an airtight lid in the refrigerator for no more than 3–4 hours.

PER 24-OUNCE SERVING		
CALORIES: 198	FAT: 0.7 G	PROTEIN: 4.2 G
SODIUM: 17 MG	FIBER: 7.9 G	
CARBOHYDRATES: 49.2 G		SUGAR: 40.6 G

ZAP POUNDS WITH ZIPPY ZUCCHINI

Vegan, Savory, Paleo

As a meal option, this smoothie combines intense flavors of filling ingredients that will provide sustainable energy and improved mental processes in a satisfying alternative to fattening, salt-laden savory entrées.

24 OUNCES

2 large kale leaves

1 small zucchini, peeled and sliced

1 cup chopped asparagus

½ small red bell pepper, seeds removed

1 small green onion, trimmed and chopped

2 small garlic cloves

2 cups water, divided

1. Combine kale, zucchini, asparagus, red pepper, onion, garlic, and 1 cup water in the 24-ounce NutriBullet cup and blend until thoroughly combined.

2. Add remaining 1 cup water and blend until combined.

3. Consume immediately or store with an airtight lid in the refrigerator for no more than 3–4 hours.

PER 24-OUNCE SERVING		
CALORIES: 82	FAT: 0.8 G	PROTEIN: 6.5 G
SODIUM: 41 MG	FIBER: 6.1 G	
CARBOHYDRATES: 16.5 G		SUGAR: 9.3 G

Vegan, Sweet, Paleo

When you're feeling dried out, tired, or just down, vitamin C–rich smoothies like this one can give you automatic energy that will pick you up and keep you going. Staying focused on your weight-loss goals is a lot easier when you feel refreshed and focused.

24 OUNCES

1 cup watercress

½ small cantaloupe, peeled and seeds removed

1 cup strawberries, tops removed

1 small orange, peeled and seeds removed

½ small lemon, peeled and seeds removed

1 cup cooled green tea, divided

1. Combine watercress, cantaloupe, strawberries, orange, lemon, and ½ cup tea in the 24-ounce NutriBullet cup and blend until thoroughly combined.

2. Add remaining ½ cup tea and blend until combined.

3. Consume immediately or store with an airtight lid in the refrigerator for no more than 3–4 hours.

PER 24–OUNCE SERVING		
CALORIES: 141	FAT: 0.5 G	PROTEIN: 3.9 G
SODIUM: 33 MG	FIBER: 7.2 G	
CARBOHYDRATES: 35.0 G		SUGAR: 25.5 G

Vitamin C Deficiencies

Even though orange juice, fresh produce, and affordable fruits and vegetables packed with vitamin C are readily available and accessible to Americans, most don't get the recommended daily value of 60 mg per day. Although multivitamins and vitamin C pill alternatives provide loads of vitamin C, the fresh sources of this important vitamin are a healthier, more refreshing option that can give you the added benefits of extra vitamins and minerals.

FLUSH OUT FAT WITH FIBER

Vegan, Sweet, Paleo

Important additions to any weight-loss diet are fruits and vegetables packed with fiber. Not only does fiber help flush out toxins and waste products from the digestive system, but it requires energy to digest. Calorie for calorie, fruits and veggies rich in fiber require more energy to digest than other foods lacking in this powerful nutrient. By consuming fiber-rich foods, you can provide your body with important vitamins and nutrients with calories that get used rather than stored.

24 OUNCES

2 large kale leaves

4 small apples, peeled, cored, and sliced

2 small carrots, peeled, sliced, and tops removed

½ small lemon, peeled and seeds removed

¼" knob ginger, peeled

3 cups cooled green tea, divided

1. Combine kale, apples, carrots, lemon, ginger, and 1½ cups tea in the 24-ounce NutriBullet cup and blend until thoroughly combined.

2. Add remaining 1½ cups tea and blend until combined.

3. Consume immediately or store with an airtight lid in the refrigerator for no more than 3–4 hours.

PER 24–OUNCE SERVING		
CALORIES: 311	FAT: 0.5 G	PROTEIN: 3.0 G
SODIUM: 78 MG	FIBER: 10.8 G	
CARBOHYDRATES: 82.0 G		SUGAR: 59.0 G

MANAGE YOUR WEIGHT WITH MANGOS

Vegan, Sweet, Paleo

Delicious and nutritious, mangos are a sweet fruit that provide loads of vitamin C and help optimize your fat-burning metabolism. This easy recipe combines only a few ingredients but delivers an amazing amount of nutrition for weight loss and total health.

24 OUNCES

1 cup watercress

2 cups peeled, pitted, and cubed mango

½ small lemon, peeled and seeds removed

¼" knob ginger, peeled

1½ cups cooled green tea, divided

1. Combine watercress, mango, lemon, ginger, and ¾ cup tea in the 24-ounce NutriBullet cup and blend until thoroughly combined.

2. Add remaining ¾ cup tea and blend until combined.

3. Consume immediately or store with an airtight lid in the refrigerator for no more than 3–4 hours.

PER 24-OUNCE SERVING		
CALORIES: 212	FAT: 1.1 G	PROTEIN: 3.8 G
SODIUM: 19 MG	FIBER: 6.3 G	
CARBOHYDRATES: 53.4 G		SUGAR: 45.9 G

SPLENDID MELON

Vegan, Sweet, Paleo

In a single serving of cantaloupe, there are a variety of vitamins and minerals that promote great health, including more than 100 percent of the recommended daily allowance (RDA) of vitamins C and A. One of the most astounding benefits of this fruit is its major role in promoting metabolism, more specifically, the metabolism of carbohydrates.

24 OUNCES

1 cup endive

1 small cantaloupe, peeled and seeds removed

1 small honeydew, peeled and seeds removed

1. Combine endive, cantaloupe, and honeydew in the 24-ounce NutriBullet cup and blend until thoroughly combined.

2. Consume immediately or store with an airtight lid in the refrigerator for no more than 3–4 hours.

PER 24-OUNCE SERVING		
CALORIES: 287	FAT: 0.8 G	PROTEIN: 5.6 G
SODIUM: 148 MG	FIBER: 8.1 G	
CARBOHYDRATES: 71.5 G		SUGAR: 63.7 G

SUPER CELERY SMOOTHIE

Vegan, Savory, Paleo

Whether you're male or female, you've felt the "bloat." Sodium, sugar, hormones, stress, diet, fluid intake, and many more factors can lead to an excessive retention of water. In order to beat the bloat, the remedy may be as easy as eating a few celery stalks! The potassium, sodium, and fiber in celery combine to effectively fight water retention.

24 OUNCES

1 cup spinach

3 celery stalks

1 small cucumber, peeled and sliced

1 small carrot, peeled, sliced, top removed

1 cup water, divided

1. Combine spinach, celery, cucumber, carrot, and ½ cup water in the 24-ounce NutriBullet cup and blend until thoroughly combined.

2. Add remaining ½ cup water and blend until combined.

3. Consume immediately or store with an airtight lid in the refrigerator for no more than 3–4 hours.

PER 24-OUNCE SERVING		
CALORIES: 63	FAT: 0.3 G	PROTEIN: 3.1 G
SODIUM: 165 MG	FIBER: 5.1 G	
CARBOHYDRATES: 12.9 G		SUGAR: 6.3 G

AHHH, SWEET GREENS!

Vegan, Sweet, Paleo

Apples and spinach in the same smoothie may seem like an unlikely pair, but one sip of this blend will have even the harshest skeptic agreeing that the duo makes a delicious treat.

24 OUNCES

1 cup spinach

2 small bananas, peeled and sliced

2 small apples, peeled, cored, and sliced

2 cups unsweetened almond milk, divided

1. Combine spinach, bananas, apples, and 1 cup almond milk in the 24-ounce NutriBullet cup and blend until thoroughly combined.

2. Add remaining 1 cup almond milk and blend until combined.

3. Consume immediately or store with an airtight lid in the refrigerator for no more than 3–4 hours.

PER 24-OUNCE SERVING		
CALORIES: 371	FAT: 5.6 G	PROTEIN: 5.8 G
SODIUM: 345 MG	FIBER: 9.3 G	
CARBOHYDRATES: 80.9 G		SUGAR: 51.5 G

Fiber Benefits

Leafy greens, vegetables, and fruits all contain some amount of this miracle substance. Fiber is beneficial because it requires more chewing time (which makes our stomachs feel fuller) and clears out our intestinal tracts (since it remains nearly intact throughout digestion). Although fiber is available in pill and powder forms, it is a far cry from a healthy bowl of spinach, broccoli, or fresh fruit.

CHAPTER 4

SMOOTHIES THAT CLEANSE AND DETOX YOUR BODY

Do you ever feel like your body just needs a break? If so, you're not alone. Cleansing and detoxification have never been more popular than they are today. And the delicious green smoothies found in this chapter will help your body flush out toxins and keep your digestive track, metabolism, and brain functioning on all cylinders as you go about your busy day.

Many people cleanse their bodies by incorporating intermittent fasting into their diets, for numerous reasons. Skipping a meal or two lets your body rest from oxidative stress or free radicals induced from foods. It is helpful for losing weight, cancer patients, and athletes. Our bodies have been accustomed to this type of eating since prehistoric days. Although the cavemen skipped meals out of necessity, our bodies are set up to function without food at certain times. This is why we have fat stores to accommodate for starvation periods.

Drinking one of the green smoothies found here helps give your body a break from solid foods, and the NutriBullet helps you transform even the most nutrient-dense smoothie into a drink that's easily absorbed and digested without taxing your system. In a sense, the NutriBullet does the digesting for you!

So make your body happy and sub out a few meals or a few days with nutrient-rich smoothies.

CLEANSING CRANBERRY

Vegan, Sweet, Paleo

If you're looking for a sweet and tangy treat, urinary tract infection relief, or both, this smoothie is for you. The combination of cranberries, cucumber, lemon, and ginger gives this smoothie the power to cleanse your body while delivering a taste sensation.

24 OUNCES

1 cup watercress

2 pints cranberries

2 small cucumbers, peeled and sliced

½ small lemon, peeled and seeds removed

½" knob ginger, peeled

2 cups water, divided

1. Combine watercress, cranberries, cucumbers, lemon, ginger, and 1 cup water in the 24-ounce NutriBullet cup and blend until thoroughly combined.

2. Add the remaining 1 cup water and blend until combined.

3. Consume immediately or store with an airtight lid in the refrigerator for no more than 3–4 hours.

PER 24-OUNCE SERVING		
CALORIES: 232	FAT: 0.4 G	PROTEIN: 4.6 G
SODIUM: 45 MG	FIBER: 21.6 G	
CARBOHYDRATES: 59.0 G		SUGAR: 21.3 G

The Cleansing Power of Cranberries

Cranberries are packed with strong antioxidants and an abundance of vitamins, minerals, and phytochemicals. Not only do these bright-red berries promote health in almost every area of the body, but they do wonders for cleansing bad bacteria out of the urinary tract while promoting an inviting environment for bladder health. Most store-bought cranberry juices contain sugary mixtures of sugars and other juices.

PAPAYA BERRY BLEND

Vegan, Sweet, Paleo

This recipe combines the crispness of romaine with the sweet flavors of papaya and strawberries to make an enjoyable blend that flushes toxins while promoting optimal health.

24 OUNCES

1 cup romaine lettuce

2 small papayas, peeled, seeded, and diced

1 cup strawberries, tops removed

1 cup water, divided

1. Combine romaine, papaya, strawberries, and ½ cup water in the 24-ounce NutriBullet cup and blend until thoroughly combined.

2. Add remaining ½ cup water and blend until combined.

3. Consume immediately or store with an airtight lid in the refrigerator for no more than 3–4 hours.

PER 24-OUNCE SERVING		
CALORIES: 188	FAT: 1.0 G	PROTEIN: 3.0 G
SODIUM: 38 MG	FIBER: 9.2 G	
CARBOHYDRATES: 46.6 G		SUGAR: 32.2 G

Eat Papaya for Overall Health

When sweetening your smoothie with papaya, it's important to note that this fruit provides an abundance of vitamins C and A. Together, these vitamins promote healthy cell growth and repair while improving the body's ability to fight off illness and disease. With the goal of detoxifying your body, fruits that provide a great source of these vitamins are a must-have in your daily diet. Papayas are a one-stop shop for both!

THE BRIGHT BLOAT BEATER

Vegan, Sweet, Paleo

With important vitamins and minerals from the watercress, strong antioxidants from the blueberries, potassium from the bananas, and vitamin C from the lemon, this smoothie is powerful in fighting free radicals and promoting overall health.

24 OUNCES

1 cup watercress

2 cups blueberries

2 small bananas, peeled and sliced

½ lemon, peeled and seeds removed

2 cups water, divided

1. Combine watercress, blueberries, bananas, lemon, and 1 cup of water in the 24-ounce NutriBullet cup and blend until thoroughly combined.

2. Add remaining 1 cup of water and blend until combined.

3. Consume immediately or store with an airtight lid in the refrigerator for no more than 3–4 hours.

PER 24-OUNCE SERVING		
CALORIES: 358	FAT: 1.1 G	PROTEIN: 5.5 G
SODIUM: 35 MG	FIBER: 13.3 G	
CARBOHYDRATES: 92.2 G		SUGAR: 55.0 G

GINGER AND APPLE CLEANSING BLEND

Vegan, Sweet, Paleo

With loads of fiber from the spinach and apples, ginger makes a star-studded appearance as a lightly spicy and aromatic addition in this recipe. It will keep your detox on track with a delightfully sweet twist.

24 OUNCES

1 cup spinach

3 small apples, peeled, cored, and sliced

½" knob ginger, peeled

2 cups water, divided

1. Combine spinach, apples, ginger, and 1 cup water in the 24-ounce NutriBullet cup and blend until thoroughly combined.

2. Add remaining 1 cup water and blend until combined.

3. Consume immediately or store with an airtight lid in the refrigerator for no more than 3–4 hours.

PER 24-OUNCE SERVING		
CALORIES: 196	FAT: 0.3 G	PROTEIN: 2.0 G
SODIUM: 41 MG	FIBER: 5.8 G	
CARBOHYDRATES: 51.8 G		SUGAR: 40.1 G

The Importance of Fiber in Cleansing

Apples are sometimes referred to as "nature's scrub brushes" because of the powerful amount of fiber they contain. Found in deep greens, vegetables, and fruits, fiber plays an important role in helping your body rid itself of waste products that may be causing irregularity. The indigestible fibers that pass through the digestive system literally sweep lingering waste with them as they leave the body. In the process of cleansing your body, moving the waste out is an important factor.

ALCOHOL RECOVERY RECIPE

Vegan, Sweet, Paleo

Although this smoothie may not relieve that pounding headache, it will definitely assist your liver in flushing out the toxins provided by alcohol consumption. This delightful blend will get your body back on track!

24 OUNCES

1 cup spinach

3 small carrots, peeled, sliced, and tops removed

2 small apples, peeled, cored, and sliced

1 small beet

2½ cups water, divided

1. Combine spinach, carrots, apples, beet, and 1¼ cups water in the 24-ounce NutriBullet cup and blend until thoroughly combined.

2. Add remaining 1¼ cups water and blend until combined.

3. Consume immediately or store with an airtight lid in the refrigerator for no more than 3–4 hours.

PER 24-OUNCE SERVING		
CALORIES: 228	FAT: 0.5 G	PROTEIN: 4.3 G
SODIUM: 212 MG	FIBER: 10.6 G	
CARBOHYDRATES: 57.0 G		SUGAR: 39.4 G

Combating the Effects of Alcohol

Because alcohol can really do a number on your liver, it is important to supply your body with the best foods to maintain your liver's optimal functioning following heavy alcohol consumption. Spinach, carrots, apples, beets, lemon, wheatgrass, and grapefruit have shown to be true superfoods when it comes to purging the liver of harmful toxins. In addition, they are also high in vitamin C and promote health while minimizing feelings of moodiness and depression.

BROCCOLI DETOX

Vegan, Sweet, Paleo

Broccoli is packed full of sulforaphane—one of the phytochemicals found in cruciferous vegetables—which stimulates the enzymes in your body. This phytochemical helps detoxify carcinogens before they damage cells.

24 OUNCES

1 cup watercress

1 cup broccoli spears

3 small red Gala apples, peeled, cored, and sliced

2 cups water, divided

1. Combine watercress, broccoli, apples, and 1 cup water in the 24-ounce NutriBullet cup and blend until thoroughly combined.

2. Add remaining 1 cup water and blend until combined.

3. Consume immediately or store with an airtight lid in the refrigerator for no more than 3–4 hours.

PER 24–OUNCE SERVING		
CALORIES: 223	FAT: 0.3 G	PROTEIN: 4.4 G
SODIUM: 61 MG	FIBER: 7.7 G	
CARBOHYDRATES: 57.0 G		SUGAR: 41.6 G

Vegan, Sweet, Paleo

This cruciferous veggie provides far more vitamins and nutrients than you would think. A single serving of broccoli includes the important vitamins A, B, C, and K along with fiber, zinc, magnesium, iron, and beta carotene.

24 OUNCES

1 cup arugula

1 cup broccoli spears

3 small apples, peeled, cored, and sliced

½ medium lemon, peeled and seeds removed

1 teaspoon coconut oil

2 cups water

1. Combine arugula, broccoli, apples, lemon, coconut oil, and water in the 24-ounce NutriBullet cup and blend until thoroughly combined.

2. Consume immediately or store with an airtight lid in the refrigerator for no more than 3–4 hours.

PER 24-OUNCE SERVING		
CALORIES: 275	FAT: 4.7 G	PROTEIN: 4.6 G
SODIUM: 53 MG	FIBER: 9.0 G	
CARBOHYDRATES: 61.2 G		SUGAR: 43.0 G

THE SPICY SAVIOR

Vegan, Savory, Paleo

The ginger in this recipe is what gives this smoothie its spicy zing! The watercress, carrots, broccoli, and ginger all combine for a filling meal replacement in any detox diet.

24 OUNCES

1 cup watercress

1 cup broccoli spears

3 carrots, peeled, sliced, and tops removed

½" knob ginger, peeled

2 cups water, divided

1. Combine watercress, broccoli, carrots, ginger, and 1 cup water in the 24-ounce NutriBullet cup and blend until thoroughly combined.

2. Add remaining 1 cup water and blend until combined.

3. Consume immediately or store with an airtight lid in the refrigerator for no more than 3–4 hours.

PER 24-OUNCE SERVING		
CALORIES: 94	FAT: 0.3 G	PROTEIN: 4.8 G
SODIUM: 164 MG	FIBER: 6.8 G	
CARBOHYDRATES: 21.1 G		SUGAR: 8.7 G

SPINACH-Y SWEET SMOOTHIE

Vegan, Sweet, Paleo

Combining spinach with deliciously sweet apples and bananas can make even the most devout spinach skeptic enjoy this nutritious rich-green veggie as a part of a detox diet.

24 OUNCES

1 cup spinach

3 small apples, peeled, cored, and sliced

2 small bananas, peeled and sliced

½ small lemon, peeled and seeds removed

2 cups water, divided

1. Combine spinach, apples, bananas, lemon, and 1 cup water in the 24-ounce NutriBullet cup and blend until thoroughly combined.

2. Add remaining 1 cup water and blend until combined.

3. Consume immediately or store with an airtight lid in the refrigerator for no more than 3–4 hours.

PER 24-OUNCE SERVING		
CALORIES: 383	FAT: 0.8 G	PROTEIN: 4.5 G
SODIUM: 43 MG	FIBER: 11.9 G	
CARBOHYDRATES: 100.5 G		SUGAR: 65.6 G

BERRIES FOR HEALTH

Vegan, Sweet, Paleo

Combining rich berries with super fruits and veggies in this recipe gives your bladder a variety of important vitamins and nutrients that will promote bladder detoxification and health!

24 OUNCES

1 cup romaine lettuce

2 cups blueberries

1 cup cranberries

1 small apple, peeled, cored, and sliced

1 small banana, peeled and sliced

½" knob ginger, peeled

2 cups water, divided

1. Combine romaine, berries, apple, banana, ginger, and 1 cup water in the 24-ounce NutriBullet cup and blend until thoroughly combined.

2. Add remaining 1 cup water and blend until combined.

3. Consume immediately or store with an airtight lid in the refrigerator for no more than 3–4 hours.

PER 24-OUNCE SERVING		
CALORIES: 373	FAT: 1.1 G	PROTEIN: 4.6 G
SODIUM: 26 MG	FIBER: 17.1 G	
CARBOHYDRATES: 96.7 G		SUGAR: 60.0 G

Berries Aren't Just for UTIs

Well-known for promoting urinary tract health, the antioxidant-rich berries in this recipe also promote a healthy bladder environment. Combining a variety of these rich berries only compounds their benefits. The berries help alleviate symptoms associated with bladder and urinary tract issues, including minimizing discomfort associated with frequent urination, bladder infections, and urinary tract infections.

CARROT CLEANSER

Vegan, Sweet, Paleo

This simple recipe takes little time to make and tastes absolutely delicious! The carrots and lemon do a complementary balancing act that provides a sweet and tangy twist.

24 OUNCES

1 cup spinach

4 small carrots, peeled, sliced, and tops removed

1 small lemon, peeled and seeds removed

2 cups water, divided

1. Combine spinach, carrots, lemon, and 1 cup water in the 24-ounce NutriBullet cup and blend until thoroughly combined.

2. Add remaining 1 cup water and blend until combined.

3. Consume immediately or store with an airtight lid in the refrigerator for no more than 3–4 hours.

PER 24-OUNCE SERVING		
CALORIES: 104	FAT: 0.4 G	PROTEIN: 3.4 G
SODIUM: 180 MG	FIBER: 7.9 G	
CARBOHYDRATES: 25.7 G		SUGAR: 11.1 G

GREEN TEA CARROT SMOOTHIE

Vegan, Sweet, Paleo

Harnessing the powerful vitamins and minerals contained in carrots while you're on a detox cleanse can help in many ways. The beta carotene that gives carrots their vibrant color is not only important for eye health; it also protects cells against free radicals and promotes optimal cell functioning.

24 OUNCES

2 cups spinach

5 small carrots, peeled, sliced, and tops removed

2 small limes, peeled and seeds removed

2 cups cooled green tea

1. Combine spinach, carrots, limes, and tea in the 24-ounce NutriBullet cup and blend until thoroughly combined.

2. Consume immediately or store with an airtight lid in the refrigerator for no more than 3–4 hours.

PER 24–OUNCE SERVING		
CALORIES: 159	FAT: 0.6 G	PROTEIN: 5.0 G
SODIUM: 225 MG	FIBER: 12.1 G	
CARBOHYDRATES: 41.3 G		SUGAR: 14.4 G

GARLIC ZUCCHINI CLEANSE

Vegan, Savory, Paleo

This savory delight is sure to cleanse your senses. Garlic is the small ingredient that makes a big impact. Not only does its flavor blend nicely with the other ingredients, but it also provides liver-cleansing health benefits.

24 OUNCES

1 cup spinach

1 small zucchini, peeled and sliced

¼ cup parsley

3 small garlic cloves

2 cups water, divided

1. Combine the spinach, zucchini, parsley, garlic, and 1 cup water in the 24-ounce NutriBullet cup and blend until thoroughly combined.

2. Add remaining 1 cup water and blend until combined.

3. Consume immediately or store with an airtight lid in the refrigerator for no more than 3–4 hours.

PER 24-OUNCE SERVING		
CALORIES: 44	FAT: 0.4 G	PROTEIN: 3.3 G
SODIUM: 59 MG	FIBER: 2.5 G	
CARBOHYDRATES: 8.9 G		SUGAR: 3.3 G

GREEN GARLIC SMOOTHIE

Vegan, Savory, Paleo

This pungent, unique smoothie will cleanse your senses and your digestive system as well. Garlic is the little powerhouse bulb that makes a big impact. Loaded with sulfur, garlic helps cleanse by producing enzymes that aid in filtering toxins and ridding the digestive tract of bacteria.

24 OUNCES

2 cups arugula

1 celery stalk, with leaves

1 small zucchini, peeled and sliced

3 small garlic cloves

2 cups cooled green tea

1. Combine arugula, celery, zucchini, garlic, and tea in the 24-ounce NutriBullet cup and blend until thoroughly combined.

2. Consume immediately or store with an airtight lid in the refrigerator for no more than 3–4 hours.

PER 24-OUNCE SERVING		
CALORIES: 66	FAT: 0.9 G	PROTEIN: 4.3 G
SODIUM: 63 MG	FIBER: 3.5 G	
CARBOHYDRATES: 12.6 G		SUGAR: 6.4 G

KALE AND CARROT FLUSH

Vegan, Sweet, Paleo

Kale provides an abundance of vitamins A and K. Combined with the iron- and folate-rich broccoli, pectin-providing apples, and beta-carotene-filled carrot, the kale makes this smoothie a completely fiber-filled one.

24 OUNCES

2 large kale leaves

1 cup broccoli spears

2 small apples, peeled, cored, and sliced

1 small carrot, peeled, sliced, and top removed

½ small lemon, peeled and seeds removed

2 cups water, divided

1. Combine kale, broccoli, apples, carrot, lemon, and 1 cup water in the 24-ounce NutriBullet cup and blend until thoroughly combined.

2. Add remaining 1 cup water and blend until combined.

3. Consume immediately or store with an airtight lid in the refrigerator for no more than 3–4 hours.

PER 24–OUNCE SERVING		
CALORIES: 187	FAT: 0.4 G	PROTEIN: 4.4 G
SODIUM: 85 MG	FIBER: 8.3 G	
CARBOHYDRATES: 47.9 G		SUGAR: 31.5 G

FIBER FLUSH SMOOTHIE

Vegan, Sweet, Paleo

With the fiber of the greens, apples, and cauliflower and the soothing effect of the ginger, this recipe utilizes the perfect combination for optimizing digestion. You can alleviate stomach discomfort with this tasty combo. Ginger is also an anti-gas aid as it relaxes tension in the gastrointestinal tract. Introduce ginger tea to your nighttime routine and you should be ready to go by morning.

24 OUNCES

1½ cups kale

¼ cup chopped cauliflower

2 small apples, peeled, cored, and sliced

½ small lime, peeled and seeds removed

½" knob ginger, peeled

2 cups cooled ginger tea

1. Combine kale, cauliflower, apples, lime, ginger, and tea in the 24-ounce NutriBullet cup and blend until thoroughly combined.

2. Consume immediately or store with an airtight lid in the refrigerator for no more than 3–4 hours.

PER 24-OUNCE SERVING		
CALORIES: 157	FAT: 0.4 G	PROTEIN: 2.5 G
SODIUM: 21 MG	FIBER: 5.8 G	
CARBOHYDRATES: 41.8 G		SUGAR: 28.2 G

COLORFUL CLEANSING COMBO

Vegan, Sweet, Paleo

This colorful combination of vegetables makes a visually and palate-pleasing creation. The ingredients provide a wealth of vitamins and minerals that will cleanse while optimizing digestive health and comfort.

24 OUNCES

1 cup watercress

3 small carrots, peeled, sliced, and tops removed

1 small cucumber, peeled and sliced

1 small beet

2 cups water, divided

1. Combine watercress, carrots, cucumber, beet, and 1 cup water in the 24-ounce NutriBullet cup and blend until thoroughly combined.

2. Add remaining 1 cup water and blend until combined.

3. Consume immediately or store with an airtight lid in the refrigerator for no more than 3–4 hours.

PER 24-OUNCE SERVING		
CALORIES: 117	FAT: 0.4 G	PROTEIN: 4.4 G
SODIUM: 200 MG	FIBER: 7.8 G	
CARBOHYDRATES: 26.1 G		SUGAR: 14.9 G

APPLE BROCCOLI DETOX BLEND

Vegan, Sweet, Paleo

Packed with fiber, vitamins, minerals, and phytochemicals that will clear out your digestive system, optimize brain functioning and mental clarity, and revitalize your body's many systems of operation, this recipe is a must-have for detox!

24 OUNCES

1 cup romaine lettuce

2 small apples, peeled, cored, and sliced

1 cup broccoli spears

1 small orange, peeled and seeds removed

2 tablespoons chopped parsley

2 cups water, divided

1. Combine romaine, apples, broccoli, orange, parsley, and 1 cup water in the 24-ounce NutriBullet cup and blend until thoroughly combined.

2. Add remaining 1 cup water and blend until combined.

3. Consume immediately or store with an airtight lid in the refrigerator for no more than 3–4 hours.

PER 24–OUNCE SERVING		
CALORIES: 210	FAT: 0.4 G	PROTEIN: 5.0 G
SODIUM: 55 MG	FIBER: 9.3 G	
CARBOHYDRATES: 53.0 G		SUGAR: 37.8 G

A GLAD GALLBLADDER

Vegan, Savory, Paleo

A cleansed gallbladder is one free of toxins and waste and able to function properly and at an optimal level. Responsible, along with the liver, for removing toxins and waste from the body, the gallbladder is an important part of the body's makeup.

24 OUNCES

1 cup spinach

1 cup chopped asparagus

½ small lemon, peeled and seeds removed

1 small tomato, sliced

1 small garlic clove

2 cups water, divided

1. Combine spinach, asparagus, lemon, tomato, garlic, and 1 cup water in the 24-ounce NutriBullet cup and blend until thoroughly combined.

2. Add remaining 1 cup water and blend until combined.

3. Consume immediately or store with an airtight lid in the refrigerator for no more than 3–4 hours.

PER 24–OUNCE SERVING		
CALORIES: 60	FAT: 0.4 G	PROTEIN: 5.1 G
SODIUM: 47 MG	FIBER: 5.4 G	
CARBOHYDRATES: 13.5 G		SUGAR: 5.8 G

Why Does Gallbladder Health Matter?

Bile acids made in the liver and used by the small intestine for breaking down foods in digestion are stored in the gallbladder. If the gallbladder isn't functioning properly, digestion can be a difficult and painful process. By promoting a healthy gallbladder, you're ensuring the digestive process moves as smoothly and regularly as possible.

CLEANSE YOUR BODY WITH SWEET CITRUS

Vegan, Sweet, Paleo

Vitamin C does more than prevent illness; it also promotes great health! This delicious combination of citrus fruits, watercress, and ginger is a delicious way to detoxify your body and promote health in one tasty treat!

24 OUNCES

1 cup watercress

1 cup peeled, cored, and cubed pineapple

1 small orange, peeled and seeds removed

1 small apple, peeled, cored, and sliced

½" knob ginger, peeled

2 cups water, divided

1. Combine watercress, pineapple, orange, apple, ginger, and 1 cup water in the 24-ounce NutriBullet cup and blend until thoroughly combined.

2. Add remaining 1 cup water and blend until combined.

3. Consume immediately or store with an airtight lid in the refrigerator for no more than 3–4 hours.

PER 24-OUNCE SERVING		
CALORIES: 193	FAT: 0.2 G	PROTEIN: 3.0 G
SODIUM: 32 MG	FIBER: 6.5 G	
CARBOHYDRATES: 50.4 G		SUGAR: 38.7 G

LIVEN UP THE LIVER

Vegan, Sweet, Paleo

The liver is a powerful organ responsible for removing unhealthy toxins from the body. Beet greens, beets, and apples are known to optimize liver functioning, and the addition of the banana's smooth texture makes this a healthy, tasty, liver-purifying blend.

24 OUNCES

1 cup beet greens

1 small beet

3 small apples, peeled, cored, and sliced

1 small banana, peeled and sliced

2 cups water, divided

1. Combine beet greens, beet, apples, banana, and 1 cup water in the 24-ounce NutriBullet cup and blend until thoroughly combined.

2. Add remaining 1 cup water and blend until combined.

3. Consume immediately or store with an airtight lid in the refrigerator for no more than 3–4 hours.

PER 24-OUNCE SERVING		
CALORIES: 322	FAT: 0.6 G	PROTEIN: 4.3 G
SODIUM: 167 MG	FIBER: 11.5 G	
CARBOHYDRATES: 83.1 G		SUGAR: 58.1 G

THE DEEP COLORS OF DETOX

Vegan, Savory, Paleo

The vibrant colors of the kale, carrot, tomato, celery, and cucumber combine with potent garlic to develop an intensely flavored, savory smoothie that provides a variety of vitamins and minerals and satisfies multiple vegetable servings in just one drink.

24 OUNCES

2 large kale leaves

1 small cucumber, peeled and sliced

2 celery stalks

1 small carrot, peeled, sliced, and top removed

1 small tomato, sliced

1 small garlic clove

2 cups water, divided

1. Combine kale, cucumber, celery, carrot, tomato, garlic, and 1 cup water in the 24-ounce NutriBullet cup and blend until thoroughly combined.

2. Add remaining 1 cup water and blend until combined.

3. Consume immediately or store with an airtight lid in the refrigerator for no more than 3–4 hours.

PER 24-OUNCE SERVING		
CALORIES: 73	FAT: 0.4 G	PROTEIN: 3.3 G
SODIUM: 126 MG	FIBER: 5.2 G	
CARBOHYDRATES: 15.8 G		SUGAR: 8.2 G

A FRUITY FLUSH

Vegan, Sweet, Paleo

Ah, the refreshing flavors of fruits with the added benefits of a cleansed body—not much can beat that! This is an easy and delicious way to satisfy cravings and fruit and vegetable servings in the same smoothie.

24 OUNCES

1 cup watercress

1 small cucumber, peeled and sliced

½ small cantaloupe, peeled and seeds removed

1 small Bartlett pear, peeled, cored, and sliced

1 small banana, peeled and sliced

2 cups water, divided

1. Combine watercress, cucumber, cantaloupe, pear, banana, and 1 cup water in the 24-ounce NutriBullet cup and blend until thoroughly combined.

2. Add remaining 1 cup water and blend until combined.

3. Consume immediately or store with an airtight lid in the refrigerator for no more than 3–4 hours.

PER 24-OUNCE SERVING		
CALORIES: 242	FAT: 1.1 G	PROTEIN: 4.3 G
SODIUM: 53 MG	FIBER: 9.6 G	
CARBOHYDRATES: 58.7 G		SUGAR: 38.0 G

REFRESHING REPRIEVE

Vegan, Sweet, Paleo

Refreshing flavors can keep a detoxifying diet on track. Calming cravings for sweets or salty foods can keep your focus on your health rather than the unhealthy alternatives.

24 OUNCES

1 cup romaine lettuce

1 small apple, peeled, cored, and sliced

1 small cucumber, peeled and sliced

1 celery stalk

1 small carrot, peeled, sliced, and top removed

1 small garlic clove

2 cups water, divided

1. Combine romaine, apple, cucumber, celery, carrot, garlic, and 1 cup water in the 24-ounce NutriBullet cup and blend until thoroughly combined.

2. Add remaining 1 cup water and blend until combined.

3. Consume immediately or store with an airtight lid in the refrigerator for no more than 3–4 hours.

PER 24-OUNCE SERVING		
CALORIES: 118	FAT: 0.3 G	PROTEIN: 2.8 G
SODIUM: 90 MG	FIBER: 5.9 G	
CARBOHYDRATES: 28.8 G		SUGAR: 19.0 G

STRAWBERRY-RHUBARB HEALING SMOOTHIE

Sweet

Strawberry and rhubarb, anyone? Yes, please! Rhubarb contains antioxidants, including lycopene and anthocyanins, which have been known to help fight cancer. It also contains a healthy amount of vitamin K, which helps your blood clot when needed and protects your bones. But one of the great benefits of rhubarb is its powerful astringency and ability to aid in cleansing and detoxification.

24 OUNCES

2 cups spinach

2 rhubarb stalks

1 cup frozen strawberries, tops removed

2 cups cooled green tea

2 tablespoons raw honey

1. Combine spinach, rhubarb, strawberries, tea, and honey in the 24-ounce NutriBullet cup and blend until thoroughly combined.

2. Consume immediately or store with an airtight lid in the refrigerator for no more than 3–4 hours.

PER 24-OUNCE SERVING		
CALORIES: 218	FAT: 0.4 G	PROTEIN: 3.5 G
SODIUM: 57 MG	FIBER: 6.3 G	
CARBOHYDRATES: 55.4 G		SUGAR: 42.2 G

GREEN CLEAN SMOOTHIE

Vegan, Sweet, Paleo

This smoothie is an easy one to remember. Just grab anything green! This drink is loaded with vitamins and minerals. As with all the recipes in this book, use this as a guide and tailor it to your taste buds and needs. If you don't have celery on hand, throw in some asparagus . . . it is all good for you and there are no wrong choices.

24 OUNCES

2 cups spinach

2 celery stalks, with leaves

2 small tart apples, peeled, cored, and sliced

2 kiwis, peeled

2 cups water

1. Combine spinach, celery, apples, kiwis, and water in the 24-ounce NutriBullet cup and blend until thoroughly combined.

2. Consume immediately or store with an airtight lid in the refrigerator for no more than 3–4 hours.

PER 24-OUNCE SERVING		
CALORIES: 243	FAT: 1.2 G	PROTEIN: 4.8 G
SODIUM: 133 MG	FIBER: 10.6 G	
CARBOHYDRATES: 60.4 G		SUGAR: 41.6 G

CHAPTER 5

SMOOTHIES FOR BETTER DIGESTIVE HEALTH

You may not know it, but your digestive system does more than move food from place to place in your body. It is actually responsible for the absorption of essential nutrients from foods, and it also regulates and disperses a variety of hormones and facilitates numerous enzymatic reactions. How can you keep this system in peak condition? NutriBullet green smoothies, of course!

In this chapter, smoothies like the Indigestion Inhibitor, Spicy Stomach Soother, and Mango Digestion Smoothie support your digestive system and ensure that fiber, vitamins, and a variety of essential minerals are readily available for use. These smoothies also help remove waste from your system and will ensure that you feel—and look—great!

INDIGESTION INHIBITOR

Vegan, Sweet, Paleo

Digestion discomfort can be painful, and the resulting gassy symptoms can be downright embarrassing. This delightful blend of sweet fruits and veggies combines with chamomile tea for a wonderful soothing effect on indigestion.

24 OUNCES

1 cup watercress

1 small carrot, peeled, sliced, and top removed

1 small apple, peeled, cored, and sliced

1 small Bartlett pear, peeled, cored, and sliced

¼" knob ginger, peeled

2 cups cooled chamomile tea, divided

1. Combine watercress, carrot, apple, pear, ginger, and 1 cup tea in the 24-ounce NutriBullet cup and blend until thoroughly combined.

2. Add remaining 1 cup tea and blend until combined.

3. Consume immediately or store with an airtight lid in the refrigerator for no more than 3–4 hours.

PER 24-OUNCE SERVING		
CALORIES: 185	FAT: 0.6 G	PROTEIN: 2.2 G
SODIUM: 52 MG	FIBER: 8.0 G	
CARBOHYDRATES: 45.9 G		SUGAR: 30.5 G

Why Fruits and Vegetables Aid Digestion

Research shows that diets high in fiber and complex carbohydrates, both found in abundance in fruits and vegetables, promote healthy digestive systems and can reduce many digestive disorders. Indigestion, ulcers, low stomach acid, constipation, diarrhea, motion sickness, colitis, and many more can be relieved or reversed with the power of produce.

PERFECT PEARS AND PINEAPPLES

Vegan, Sweet, Paleo

The amazing flavors of pineapples and pears are enhanced by the addition of lemon in this recipe. With abundant vitamins and minerals that act to aid in digestion and prevent discomfort, this is a splendid blend for any indigestion sufferer.

24 OUNCES

1 cup romaine lettuce

2 cups peeled, cored, and cubed pineapple

2 small Bartlett pears, peeled, cored, and sliced

1 small lemon, peeled and seeds removed

2 cups cooled chamomile tea, divided

1. Combine romaine, pineapple, pears, lemon, and 1 cup of tea in the 24-ounce NutriBullet cup and blend until thoroughly combined.

2. Add remaining 1 cup tea and blend until combined.

3. Consume immediately or store with an airtight lid in the refrigerator for no more than 3–4 hours.

PER 24–OUNCE SERVING		
CALORIES: 383	FAT: 1.2 G	PROTEIN: 4.2 G
SODIUM: 14 MG	FIBER: 16.7 G	
CARBOHYDRATES: 96.8 G		SUGAR: 64.0 G

AMAZING APPLES FOR DIGESTION

Vegan, Sweet, Paleo

Apples star in this delightful recipe because of their high fiber content. With the added benefits from pineapple's vitamin C stores, this combination of deep greens, vibrant fruits, and chamomile tea will make for a digestive system that performs at peak functioning!

24 OUNCES

1 cup watercress

3 small apples, peeled, cored, and sliced

1 cup peeled, cored, and cubed pineapple

¼" knob ginger, peeled

2 cups cooled chamomile tea, divided

1. Combine watercress, apples, pineapple, ginger, and 1 cup tea in the 24-ounce NutriBullet cup and blend until thoroughly combined.

2. Add remaining 1 cup tea and blend until combined.

3. Consume immediately or store with an airtight lid in the refrigerator for no more than 3–4 hours.

PER 24-OUNCE SERVING		
CALORIES: 279	FAT: 0.3 G	PROTEIN: 2.8 G
SODIUM: 18 MG	FIBER: 7.6 G	
CARBOHYDRATES: 73.7 G		SUGAR: 56.3 G

DREAMY DIGESTION

Vegan, Sweet, Paleo

On the uncomfortable nights that indigestion creeps up, turn to your NutriBullet for quick relief. This delightfully sweet fruit and veggie combination provides indigestion relief in one sweet treat you can enjoy as dessert or right when the burn hits!

24 OUNCES

1 cup romaine lettuce

2 small apples, peeled, cored, and sliced

2 small carrots, peeled, sliced, and tops removed

1 small cucumber, peeled and sliced

½ small lemon, peeled and seeds removed

2 cups cooled chamomile tea, divided

1. Combine romaine, apples, carrots, cucumber, lemon, and 1 cup tea in the 24-ounce NutriBullet cup and blend until thoroughly combined.

2. Add remaining 1 cup tea and blend until combined.

3. Consume immediately or store with an airtight lid in the refrigerator for no more than 3–4 hours.

PER 24-OUNCE SERVING		
CALORIES: 204	FAT: 0.5 G	PROTEIN: 3.5 G
SODIUM: 79 MG	FIBER: 9.1 G	
CARBOHYDRATES: 51.9 G		SUGAR: 34.9 G

A Recipe for Sweet Dreams

Indigestion can strike at any time of day, but can be especially uncomfortable at night and can lead to painful discomfort, interrupted sleep, and moodiness. Taking a two-step approach may help: 1) Use fruit and vegetable combinations shown to regulate stomach acid and promote more alkaline levels of the digestive tract, and 2) drink chamomile tea before bed. Chamomile tea has been shown to aid in indigestion by soothing the esophageal muscles and those of the large and small intestine.

PINEAPPLE-PAPAYA PROTECTION

Vegan, Sweet, Paleo

Although an important ingredient, the romaine's taste is almost completely masked by the flavorful fruit combination in this recipe. This recipe not only protects the stomach lining, but it is an amazing treat to be enjoyed whenever the craving for fruit strikes!

24 OUNCES

1 cup romaine lettuce

2 cups peeled, cored, and cubed pineapple

2 cups peeled, seeded, and diced papaya

½ small lemon, peeled and seeds removed

¼" knob ginger, peeled

2 cups cooled chamomile tea, divided

1. Combine romaine, pineapple, papaya, lemon, ginger, and 1 cup tea in the 24-ounce NutriBullet cup and blend until thoroughly combined.

2. Add remaining 1 cup tea and blend until combined.

3. Consume immediately or store with an airtight lid in the refrigerator for no more than 3–4 hours.

PER 24-OUNCE SERVING		
CALORIES: 308	FAT: 0.9 G	PROTEIN: 4.1 G
SODIUM: 33 MG	FIBER: 11.4 G	
CARBOHYDRATES: 80.0 G		SUGAR: 56.5 G

CUCUMBER COOLER

Vegan, Sweet, Paleo

The refreshing combination of sweet citrus, crisp greens, zippy ginger, and cooling cucumbers will perk you up while cooling your tummy. Indigestion stands no chance against the chilling effects of this cool combo.

24 OUNCES

1 cup watercress

1 small pink grapefruit, peeled and seeds removed

1 small orange, peeled and seeds removed

2 small cucumbers, peeled and sliced

¼" knob ginger, peeled

2 cups cooled chamomile tea, divided

1. Combine watercress, grapefruit, orange, cucumbers, ginger, and 1 cup tea in the 24-ounce NutriBullet cup and blend until thoroughly combined.

2. Add remaining 1 cup tea and blend until combined.

3. Consume immediately or store with an airtight lid in the refrigerator for no more than 3–4 hours.

PER 24-OUNCE SERVING		
CALORIES: 217	FAT: 0.3 G	PROTEIN: 6.1 G
SODIUM: 23 MG	FIBER: 9.1 G	
CARBOHYDRATES: 51.9 G		SUGAR: 41.3 G

GINGER ALE SMOOTHIE

Vegan, Sweet, Paleo

Ginger ale is the most common remedy for any type of stomach ailment. This natural version of ginger ale provides all of the powerful nutrition without the sometimes uncomfortable and problematic carbonation.

24 OUNCES

1 cup watercress

4 small apples, peeled, cored, and sliced

¼" knob ginger, peeled

2 cups cooled chamomile tea, divided

1. Combine watercress, apples, ginger, and 1 cup tea in the 24-ounce NutriBullet cup and blend until thoroughly combined.

2. Add remaining 1 cup tea and blend until combined.

3. Consume immediately or store with an airtight lid in the refrigerator for no more than 3–4 hours.

PER 24-OUNCE SERVING		
CALORIES: 260	FAT: 0.3 G	PROTEIN: 2.2 G
SODIUM: 17 MG	FIBER: 7.1 G	
CARBOHYDRATES: 68.9 G		SUGAR: 53.4 G

SMOOTH CITRUS FOR SMOOTH DIGESTION

Vegan, Sweet, Paleo

A delicious remedy for stomach discomfort, this banana blend is a much sweeter and nutritious alternative to an over-the-counter antacid.

24 OUNCES

1 cup watercress

2 cups peeled, cored, and cubed pineapple

1 small peach, pitted and peeled

1 small orange, peeled and seeds removed

2 small bananas, peeled and sliced

2 cups cooled chamomile tea, divided

1. Combine watercress, pineapple, peach, orange, bananas, and 1 cup tea in the 24-ounce NutriBullet cup and blend until thoroughly combined.

2. Add remaining 1 cup tea and blend until combined.

3. Consume immediately or store with an airtight lid in the refrigerator for no more than 3–4 hours.

PER 24-OUNCE SERVING		
CALORIES: 446	FAT: 0.9 G	PROTEIN: 6.9 G
SODIUM: 22 MG	FIBER: 14.3 G	
CARBOHYDRATES: 114.5 G		SUGAR: 77.2 G

SWEET FIBER

Vegan, Sweet, Paleo

Apricots, apples, and bananas blend with sweet romaine for a delicious fiber-rich treat that will promote optimal digestion. The uncomfortable symptoms of indigestion can also be alleviated with deep greens like romaine.

24 OUNCES

1 cup romaine lettuce

4 small apricots, peeled and pitted

2 small apples, peeled, cored, and sliced

1 small banana, peeled and sliced

2 cups cooled chamomile tea, divided

1. Combine romaine, apricots, apples, banana, and 1 cup tea in the 24-ounce NutriBullet cup and blend until thoroughly combined.

2. Add remaining 1 cup tea and blend until combined.

3. Consume immediately or store with an airtight lid in the refrigerator for no more than 3–4 hours.

PER 24-OUNCE SERVING		
CALORIES: 293	FAT: 0.8 G	PROTEIN: 4.4 G
SODIUM: 9 MG	FIBER: 9.8 G	
CARBOHYDRATES: 74.8 G		SUGAR: 52.5 G

Fabulous Fiber

Fiber is absolutely necessary to promote the most efficient digestive system free of toxins, waste, and buildup that may have accrued over the years. Stock up on fiber-rich foods and blend them in delicious smoothies. Not only does blending the fiber-packed fruits and veggies make for delicious meal and snack options, but blending them breaks down the indigestible fiber for the best possible absorption.

PEARS, APPLES, AND GINGER

Vegan, Sweet, Paleo

There's not much that can compare to the sweet combination of pears, apples, and ginger. This scrumptious blend comforts your stomach with balanced nutrition in every glass.

24 OUNCES

1 cup watercress

3 small apples, peeled, cored, and sliced

3 small Bartlett pears, peeled, cored, and sliced

¼" knob ginger, peeled

2 cups cooled chamomile tea, divided

1. Combine watercress, apples, pears, ginger, and 1 cup tea in the 24-ounce NutriBullet cup and blend until thoroughly combined.

2. Add remaining 1 cup tea and blend until combined.

3. Consume immediately or store with an airtight lid in the refrigerator for no more than 3–4 hours.

PER 24-OUNCE SERVING		
CALORIES: 481	FAT: 1.3 G	PROTEIN: 2.7 G
SODIUM: 17 MG	FIBER: 19.3 G	
CARBOHYDRATES: 120.0 G		SUGAR: 84.2 G

Fiber Effects of Pears

Since fiber promotes a more optimal functioning digestive tract, why not enjoy a green smoothie that packs a whopping amount of fiber from greens, pears, and apples? This delicious smoothie can get your digestive system working at its full potential and make regularity a regular occurrence every day!

MOVE OVER, MOTION SICKNESS!

Vegan, Sweet, Paleo

Cabbage is a little-known combatant for motion sickness. Blending the green leafy veggie with bananas, apples, and ginger makes for a delicious remedy to this day-wrecking condition!

24 OUNCES

1 cup cabbage

3 small bananas, peeled and sliced

2 small apples, peeled, cored, and sliced

¼" knob ginger, peeled

2 cups cooled chamomile tea, divided

1. Combine cabbage, bananas, apples, ginger, and 1 cup tea in the 24-ounce NutriBullet cup and blend until thoroughly combined.

2. Add remaining 1 cup tea and blend until combined.

3. Consume immediately or store with an airtight lid in the refrigerator for no more than 3–4 hours.

PER 24–OUNCE SERVING		
CALORIES: 421	FAT: 0.8 G	PROTEIN: 5.2 G
SODIUM: 23 MG	FIBER: 13.6 G	
CARBOHYDRATES: 109.1 G		SUGAR: 66.6 G

Vegan, Savory, Paleo

A tasty way to combat heartburn and provide fast-acting relief, this smoothie combines flavorful veggies that will soothe your esophagus and relieve the pain associated with acid indigestion.

24 OUNCES

1 cup spinach

3 celery stalks, with leaves

1½ cups cooled chamomile tea, divided

1. Combine spinach, celery, and ¾ cup tea in the 24-ounce NutriBullet cup and blend until thoroughly combined.

2. Add remaining ¾ cup tea and blend until combined.

3. Consume immediately or store with an airtight lid in the refrigerator for no more than 3–4 hours.

PER 24-OUNCE SERVING		
CALORIES: 28	FAT: 0.2 G	PROTEIN: 1.7 G
SODIUM: 122 MG	FIBER: 2.6 G	
CARBOHYDRATES: 5.4 G		SUGAR: 1.7 G

Lifestyle Changes for Heartburn Relief

Not much can compare to the potentially disabling condition of acid reflux. Many people find themselves popping antacids and heartburn relievers numerous times throughout the day just to make the discomfort subside. A great way to combat this debilitating condition is to change your diet to include a wide variety of fruits and vegetables while cutting out caffeine, cigarettes, alcohol, fatty and acidic foods, and carbonation.

SPICY STOMACH SOOTHER

Vegan, Savory, Paleo

Spicy arugula and crisp veggies with a bite offer up a deliciously savory taste combination that will soothe your stomach while calming cravings for harsh, spicy foods that could aggravate digestion and lead to discomfort.

24 OUNCES

1 cup arugula

1 small green onion, trimmed and chopped

3 celery stalks

1 small garlic clove

2 cups cooled chamomile tea, divided

1. Combine arugula, onion, celery, garlic, and 1 cup tea in the 24-ounce NutriBullet cup and blend until thoroughly combined.

2. Add remaining 1 cup tea and blend until combined.

3. Consume immediately or store with an airtight lid in the refrigerator for no more than 3–4 hours.

PER 24-OUNCE SERVING		
CALORIES: 33	FAT: 0.3 G	PROTEIN: 1.6 G
SODIUM: 105 MG	FIBER: 2.4 G	
CARBOHYDRATES: 6.6 G		SUGAR: 2.2 G

GET RID OF GAS!

Vegan, Savory, Paleo

Gas is possibly one of the most embarrassing symptoms associated with indigestion and digestive disorders. Gas-fighting foods are combined in this delicious smoothie.

24 OUNCES

1 cup spinach

2 small carrots, peeled, sliced, and tops removed

3 celery stalks, with leaves

¾ cup green beans

2 cups cooled chamomile tea, divided

1. Combine spinach, carrots, celery, green beans, and 1 cup tea in the 24-ounce NutriBullet cup and blend until thoroughly combined.

2. Add remaining 1 cup tea and blend until combined.

3. Consume immediately or store with an airtight lid in the refrigerator for no more than 3–4 hours.

PER 24-OUNCE SERVING		
CALORIES: 93	FAT: 0.5 G	PROTEIN: 4.0 G
SODIUM: 196 MG	FIBER: 7.9 G	
CARBOHYDRATES: 20.4 G		SUGAR: 6.5 G

TUMMY PROTECTOR

Vegan, Savory, Paleo

A savory way to coat your sensitive stomach is with delicious vegetables like these. Romaine, celery, green onion, tomatoes, and comforting mild chamomile tea deliver comfort and protection in every delicious sip.

24 OUNCES

1 cup romaine lettuce

3 celery stalks, with leaves

1 small green onion, trimmed and chopped

2 small tomatoes, sliced

2 cups cooled chamomile tea, divided

1. Combine romaine, celery, onion, tomatoes, and 1 cup tea in the 24-ounce NutriBullet cup and blend until thoroughly combined.

2. Add remaining 1 cup tea and blend until combined.

3. Consume immediately or store with an airtight lid in the refrigerator for no more than 3–4 hours.

PER 24-OUNCE SERVING		
CALORIES: 63	FAT: 0.5 G	PROTEIN: 3.1 G
SODIUM: 112 MG	FIBER: 5.2 G	
CARBOHYDRATES: 13.5 G		SUGAR: 7.1 G

Vegan, Savory, Paleo

Rich in beta carotene, a powerful antioxidant, red pepper acts to protect your digestive tract from dangerous cancers while also providing rich vitamins and minerals that make for happy digestion.

24 OUNCES

1 cup romaine lettuce

1 small red bell pepper, top and seeds removed, ribs intact

2 celery stalks, with leaves

½ small lemon, peeled and seeds removed

1½ cups cooled chamomile tea, divided

1. Combine romaine, red pepper, celery, lemon, and ¾ cup tea in the 24-ounce NutriBullet cup and blend until thoroughly combined.

2. Add remaining ¾ cup tea and blend until combined.

3. Consume immediately or store with an airtight lid in the refrigerator for no more than 3–4 hours.

PER 24-OUNCE SERVING		
CALORIES: 52	FAT: 0.3 G	PROTEIN: 2.2 G
SODIUM: 72 MG	FIBER: 4.6 G	
CARBOHYDRATES: 11.8 G		SUGAR: 5.5 G

KEEP IT MOVING

Vegan, Savory, Paleo

Flavorful spinach and zucchini make for a splendid blend with the fresh but lightly flavored celery. Wonderfully light and delicious, this is a smoothie that will not only taste great but will also relieve constipation and alleviate the uncomfortable symptoms that result!

24 OUNCES

1 cup spinach

2 small zucchini, peeled and sliced

3 celery stalks, with leaves

2 cups cooled chamomile tea, divided

1. Combine spinach, zucchini, celery, and 1 cup tea in the 24-ounce NutriBullet cup and blend until thoroughly combined.

2. Add remaining 1 cup tea and blend until combined.

3. Consume immediately or store with an airtight lid in the refrigerator for no more than 3–4 hours.

PER 24–OUNCE SERVING		
CALORIES: 95	FAT: 1.4 G	PROTEIN: 6.5 G
SODIUM: 155 MG	FIBER: 6.6 G	
CARBOHYDRATES: 17.6 G		SUGAR: 11.5 G

Produce for Constipation Relief

Constipation can really slow you down! The irritating condition can make you feel lethargic, uncomfortable, and irritable. Stay regular by including the recommended 5 servings of fruits and veggies daily. All of this produce contains lots of fiber, which relieves constipation.

CABBAGE CALMS INDIGESTION

Vegan, Savory, Paleo

This delightful combination of cabbage and cruciferous veggies packs a punch in providing rich vitamins and minerals, and it aids in digestion with its rich sources of vitamin K and carotenes that combine to act as an anti-inflammatory.

24 OUNCES

1 cup cabbage

1 cup broccoli spears

1 cup chopped cauliflower

1 small garlic clove

2 cups cooled chamomile tea, divided

1. Combine cabbage, broccoli, cauliflower, garlic, and 1 cup tea in the 24-ounce NutriBullet cup and blend until thoroughly combined.

2. Add remaining 1 cup tea and blend until combined.

3. Consume immediately or store with an airtight lid in the refrigerator for no more than 3–4 hours.

PER 24-OUNCE SERVING		
CALORIES: 81	FAT: 0.3 G	PROTEIN: 5.7 G
SODIUM: 78 MG	FIBER: 6.3 G	
CARBOHYDRATES: 17.4 G		SUGAR: 5.9 G

MEGA MAGNESIUM

Vegan, Savory, Paleo

With powerful stores of minerals, especially magnesium, the veggies in this recipe promote easier digestion along with overall health for your entire body and mind.

24 OUNCES

1 cup cabbage

1 cup broccoli spears

1 cup chopped cauliflower

2 celery stalks, with leaves

2 cups cooled chamomile tea, divided

1. Combine cabbage, broccoli, cauliflower, celery, and 1 cup tea in the 24-ounce NutriBullet cup and blend until thoroughly combined.

2. Add remaining 1 cup tea and blend until combined.

3. Consume immediately or store with an airtight lid in the refrigerator for no more than 3–4 hours.

PER 24-OUNCE SERVING		
CALORIES: 89	FAT: 0.4 G	PROTEIN: 6.1 G
SODIUM: 142 MG	FIBER: 7.5 G	
CARBOHYDRATES: 18.7 G		SUGAR: 6.9 G

Magnesium Benefits

This powerful mineral is responsible for the proper functioning of our muscles and nerves, so it is very important to men and women at any age and any lifestyle. Deficiencies in magnesium can lead to debilitating conditions like diabetes, hypertension, osteoporosis, and irritable bowel syndrome. It can also negatively affect digestion by reducing its natural calming effect on muscle spasms and impairing the strength of the muscles associated with digestion.

THE CONSTIPATION CURE

Vegan, Savory, Paleo

Cure the most uncomfortable indigestion symptoms like constipation with delicious smoothies like this one, which features a delicious blend of savory and crisp vegetables.

24 OUNCES

1 cup romaine lettuce

1 cup chopped asparagus

1 cup broccoli spears

2 small carrots, peeled, sliced, and tops removed

2 cups cooled chamomile tea, divided

1. Combine romaine, asparagus, broccoli, carrots, and 1 cup tea in the 24-ounce NutriBullet cup and blend until thoroughly combined.

2. Add remaining 1 cup tea and blend until combined.

3. Consume immediately or store with an airtight lid in the refrigerator for no more than 3–4 hours.

PER 24-OUNCE SERVING		
CALORIES: 108	FAT: 0.4 G	PROTEIN: 7.0 G
SODIUM: 108 MG	FIBER: 9.0 G	
CARBOHYDRATES: 23.3 G		SUGAR: 9.4 G

COOL OFF COLITIS

Vegan, Savory, Paleo

Remedy this terrible digestive disorder with vegetables rich in vitamin E! Spinach, asparagus, carrots, tomato, and light chamomile make for a savory, yet slightly sweet, smoothie.

24 OUNCES

1 cup spinach

1 cup chopped asparagus

3 small carrots, peeled, sliced, and tops removed

1 small tomato, sliced

2 cups cooled chamomile tea, divided

1. Combine spinach, asparagus, carrots, tomato, and 1 cup tea in the 24-ounce NutriBullet cup and blend until thoroughly combined.

2. Add remaining 1 cup tea and blend until combined.

3. Consume immediately or store with an airtight lid in the refrigerator for no more than 3–4 hours.

PER 24-OUNCE SERVING		
CALORIES: 113	FAT: 0.5 G	PROTEIN: 6.0 G
SODIUM: 136 MG	FIBER: 8.8 G	
CARBOHYDRATES: 25.2 G		SUGAR: 12.2 G

MANGO DIGESTION SMOOTHIE

Vegan, Sweet, Paleo

Mangos aid digestion by combating acidity and uncomfortable acids in the digestive system; they create a more placid, balanced system and promote a smooth, regular digestive process. The apple and the arugula in this smoothie are high in fiber, and the coconut water is full of electrolytes that will keep your body hydrated and prevent constipation.

24 OUNCES

2 cups arugula

1½ cups frozen mango cubes

1 small apple, peeled, cored, and sliced

½" knob ginger, peeled

2 cups coconut water

1. Combine arugula, mangos, apple, ginger, and coconut water in the 24-ounce NutriBullet cup and blend until thoroughly combined.

2. Consume immediately or store with an airtight lid in the refrigerator for no more than 3–4 hours.

PER 24-OUNCE SERVING		
CALORIES: 341	FAT: 0.3 G	PROTEIN: 2.5 G
SODIUM: 137 MG	FIBER: 6.4 G	
CARBOHYDRATES: 87.3 G		SUGAR: 75.4 G

BEANY SPINACH

Vegan, Savory, Paleo

You would think that such a spicy addition would cause stomach discomfort, but the cayenne pepper in this smoothie has amazing benefits. Cayenne has the ability to promote a digestive enzyme that works to kill bad bacteria ingested from foods while also promoting the good bacteria that optimizes the digestive process. As if that wasn't enough, these hot little items also work so hard to fight off bad bacteria they actually prevent stomach ulcers!

24 OUNCES

1 cup spinach

1 cup canned red kidney beans, rinsed and drained

1 cup canned great northern beans, rinsed and drained

½ teaspoon cayenne pepper

2 cups water, divided

1. Combine spinach, beans, cayenne pepper, and 1 cup water in the 24-ounce NutriBullet cup and blend until thoroughly combined.

2. Add remaining 1 cup water and blend until combined.

3. Consume immediately or store with an airtight lid in the refrigerator for no more than 3–4 hours.

PER 24-OUNCE SERVING		
CALORIES: 383	FAT: 2.2 G	PROTEIN: 26.3 G
SODIUM: 771 MG	FIBER: 23.9 G	
CARBOHYDRATES: 72.7 G		SUGAR: 5.0 G

AN APPLE PIE DAY

Vegan, Sweet, Paleo

The cloves and cinnamon in this smoothie add a flavor reminiscent of apple pie and add to the health benefits already present in the spinach, apples, and CoconutMilk. The fiber alone can help your body feel regular and well adjusted throughout the day!

24 OUNCES

2 cups spinach

1 teaspoon ground cloves

1 teaspoon cinnamon

3 small apples, peeled, cored, and sliced

1½ cups unsweetened CoconutMilk

1. Layer the spinach in the NutriBullet's 24-ounce cup.

2. Add the spices followed by the apples, then add the milk.

3. Blend until thoroughly combined.

4. Consume immediately or store with an airtight lid in the refrigerator for no more than 3–4 hours.

PER 24-OUNCE SERVING		
CALORIES: 281	FAT: 6.6 G	PROTEIN: 3.0 G
SODIUM: 104 MG	FIBER: 8.6 G	
CARBOHYDRATES: 56.2 G		SUGAR: 40.4 G

The Surprising Power of Cloves

Although most consider cloves an essential when it comes time to make pies for the holidays, Ayurvedic healers utilize this spice for its healing powers—it's believed to alleviate symptoms of irregular digestion and malfunctioning metabolism. Although it is used in only small amounts, it's antibacterial and antiviral properties in any amount can't hurt!

PLEASANTLY PEAR

Vegan, Sweet, Paleo

Fiber helps keep your digestive tract functioning optimally. Why not enjoy a green smoothie that packs a whopping amount of fiber from greens, pears, and apples? This delicious smoothie can get your digestive system working at its full potential and make irregularity a thing of the past.

24 OUNCES

1 cup romaine lettuce

2 small Bartlett pears, peeled, cored, and sliced

1 small apple, peeled, cored, and sliced

1 small banana, peeled and sliced

½ cup water, divided

1. Combine romaine, pears, apple, banana, and ¼ cup water in the 24-ounce NutriBullet cup and blend thoroughly.

2. Add remaining water and blend until combined.

3. Consume immediately or store with an airtight lid in the refrigerator for no more than 3–4 hours.

PER 24-OUNCE SERVING		
CALORIES: 350	FAT: 1.1 G	PROTEIN: 3.2 G
SODIUM: 11 MG	FIBER: 14.8 G	
CARBOHYDRATES: 87.1 G		SUGAR: 55.7 G

MINTY MADNESS

Vegan, Sweet

Mint gums that make your mouth feel clean and your breath taste fresh are not the only great contribution this wonderful herb has given humanity. As an herb with strong antiseptic, antibacterial, and antifungal properties, mint has the ability to calm the stomach and digestive system. Stomachaches, irregularity, and irritable bowel syndrome can all be aided with the use of mint.

24 OUNCES

1 cup iceberg lettuce

½ cup mint leaves

1 small cucumber, peeled and sliced

1 cup rice milk, divided

1. Combine the iceberg, mint, cucumber, and ½ cup rice milk in the 24-ounce NutriBullet cup and blend until thoroughly combined.

2. Add remaining rice milk and blend until combined.

3. Consume immediately or store with an airtight lid in the refrigerator for no more than 3–4 hours.

PER 24-OUNCE SERVING		
CALORIES: 153	FAT: 2.7 G	PROTEIN: 2.9 G
SODIUM: 111 MG	FIBER: 2.8 G	
CARBOHYDRATES: 31.0 G		SUGAR: 14.3 G

MANGO BERRY

Vegan, Sweet, Paleo

The fresh fruits found in this delicious Mango Berry green smoothie will give you a boost, no matter the time of day, and creating this smoothie in the NutriBullet means that you'll be able to digest them without any issues. Enjoy!

24 OUNCES

1 cup watercress

2 small mangos, pitted and peeled

2 pints raspberries

1½ cups unsweetened CoconutMilk, divided

1. Combine watercress, mangos, raspberries, and ¾ cup CoconutMilk in the 24-ounce NutriBullet cup and blend until thoroughly combined.

2. Add remaining CoconutMilk and blend until combined.

3. Consume immediately or store with an airtight lid in the refrigerator for no more than 3–4 hours.

PER 24-OUNCE SERVING		
CALORIES: 622	FAT: 9.7 G	PROTEIN: 10.8 G
SODIUM: 73 MG	FIBER: 40.1 G	
CARBOHYDRATES: 133.0 G		SUGAR: 89.4 G

GINGER APPLE

Vegan, Sweet, Paleo

The fiber from the romaine and apples offers the benefit of an optimal digestive system, and the ginger soothes any stomach discomfort. This recipe is highly recommended for those days you may feel especially irregular or uncomfortable.

24 OUNCES

1 cup romaine lettuce

3 small apples, peeled, cored, and sliced

¼" knob garlic, peeled

2 cups unsweetened almond milk, divided

1. Combine romaine, apples, ginger, and 1 cup almond milk in the 24-ounce NutriBullet cup and blend until thoroughly combined.

2. Add remaining 1 cup almond milk and blend until combined.

3. Consume immediately or store with an airtight lid in the refrigerator for no more than 3–4 hours.

PER 24–OUNCE SERVING		
CALORIES: 257	FAT: 5.3 G	PROTEIN: 3.7 G
SODIUM: 323 MG	FIBER: 6.2 G	
CARBOHYDRATES: 52.2 G		SUGAR: 40.6 G

Fiber and Ginger Combination

Ginger is hailed as one of nature's most potent medicinal plants, with its most well-known cure being for stomach ailments. Combining ginger with the fiber found in fruits and leafy greens is an effective way to clean out the digestive tract, promote the release of good digestive enzymes, and soothe the stomach.

CHAPTER 6

SMOOTHIES FOR ANTIAGING, BETTER SKIN, AND BODY CARE

The processed foods that line the aisles of the grocery store are aging us. But the green smoothies found in this chapter are a virtual fountain of youth! Recipes for smoothies like Calming Cucumber, Backwards Berry, and Antioxidant Assist made in your NutriBullet give you a variety of nutrients and phytochemicals in one meal, which aid in cell function, repair your skin and bones, maintain mental clarity, help protect against cancers, and restore and maintain your youthfulness—inside and out!

SPICY REFRESHMENT

Vegan, Sweet, Paleo

Spicy arugula gets sweetened up a bit with pears, grapes, and zippy ginger to make a wonderful smoothie. This recipe is full of vitamins, minerals, and antioxidants that provide total health, beautiful eyes, and luxurious skin.

24 OUNCES

1 cup arugula

4 small Bartlett pears, peeled, cored, and sliced

1 cup red grapes

½" knob ginger, peeled

2 cups cooled chamomile tea, divided

1. Combine arugula, pears, grapes, ginger, and 1 cup tea in the 24-ounce NutriBullet cup and blend until thoroughly combined.

2. Add remaining 1 cup tea and blend until combined.

3. Consume immediately or store with an airtight lid in the refrigerator for no more than 3–4 hours.

PER 24–OUNCE SERVING		
CALORIES: 496	FAT: 1.4 G	PROTEIN: 4.0 G
SODIUM: 18 MG	FIBER: 20.6 G	
CARBOHYDRATES: 120.5 G		SUGAR: 82.7 G

Balanced Diet for Better Skin

Crash dieting is a definite no-no when trying to clear up acne! Studies have shown that extreme changes in diet like the total avoidance of fats or excessive inclusion of fats as the sole source of food can destabilize the amount of secretions of the pores, which is the major source of acne. Include a variety of fresh fruits and veggies with little fats to promote the most balanced environment for beautiful skin!

BONE UP WITH BLACKBERRIES

Vegan, Sweet, Paleo

Rich vitamins and minerals that will optimize all those steps you take for optimal health are abundant in this smoothie recipe.

24 OUNCES

1 cup watercress

2 cups blackberries

2 small bananas, peeled and sliced

2 small oranges, peeled and seeds removed

2 cups cooled chamomile tea, divided

1. Combine watercress, blackberries, bananas, oranges, and 1 cup tea in the 24-ounce NutriBullet cup and blend until thoroughly combined.

2. Add remaining 1 cup tea and blend until combined.

3. Consume immediately or store with an airtight lid in the refrigerator for no more than 3–4 hours.

PER 24-OUNCE SERVING		
CALORIES: 399	FAT: 1.5 G	PROTEIN: 8.8 G
SODIUM: 21 MG	FIBER: 25.3 G	
CARBOHYDRATES: 97.8 G		SUGAR: 56.8 G

BACKWARDS BERRY

Vegan, Sweet, Paleo

Beautiful, healthier, more hydrated skin and hair are added benefits from this smoothie. The antioxidants provided protect against free-radical damage that can wreak havoc on the inside and outside of your body.

24 OUNCES

1 cup spinach

1 pint blackberries

1 pint raspberries

¼" knob ginger, peeled

½ small lemon, peeled and seeds removed

2 cups cooled chamomile tea, divided

1. Combine spinach, berries, ginger, lemon, and 1 cup tea in the 24-ounce NutriBullet cup and blend until thoroughly combined.

2. Add remaining 1 cup tea and blend until combined.

3. Consume immediately or store with an airtight lid in the refrigerator for no more than 3–4 hours.

PER 24–OUNCE SERVING		
CALORIES: 268	FAT: 2.1 G	PROTEIN: 8.1 G
SODIUM: 31 MG	FIBER: 32.7 G	
CARBOHYDRATES: 61.9 G		SUGAR: 25.8 G

DOUBLE-DUTY DELIGHT

Vegan, Sweet, Paleo

Luscious fruits like papaya, pineapple, and strawberries make for the perfect blend with delicious vitamin- and mineral-rich romaine. This smoothie's powerful antioxidants will make you look and feel younger.

24 OUNCES

1 cup romaine lettuce

1 cup peeled, seeded, and diced papaya

1 cup peeled, cored, and cubed pineapple

1 pint strawberries, tops removed

2 cups cooled chamomile tea, divided

1. Combine romaine, papaya, pineapple, strawberries, and 1 cup tea in the 24-ounce NutriBullet cup and blend until thoroughly combined.

2. Add remaining 1 cup tea and blend until combined.

3. Consume immediately or store with an airtight lid in the refrigerator for no more than 3–4 hours.

PER 24-OUNCE SERVING		
CALORIES: 247	FAT: 1.1 G	PROTEIN: 4.1 G
SODIUM: 21 MG	FIBER: 11.5 G	
CARBOHYDRATES: 62.0 G		SUGAR: 42.2 G

GRAPPLEBERRY

Vegan, Sweet, Paleo

Morning, noon, or night, you can enjoy this delightful treat packed with powerful nutrition. Promoting total health on the inside and out, this recipe provides balanced nutrition for any and all health issues.

24 OUNCES

1 cup watercress

1 cup red seedless grapes

2 small apples, peeled, cored, and sliced

1 pint raspberries

2 cups cooled chamomile tea, divided

1. Combine watercress, grapes, apples, raspberries, and 1 cup tea in the 24-ounce NutriBullet cup and blend until thoroughly combined.

2. Add remaining 1 cup tea and blend until combined.

3. Consume immediately or store with an airtight lid in the refrigerator for no more than 3–4 hours.

PER 24-OUNCE SERVING		
CALORIES: 364	FAT: 1.4 G	PROTEIN: 5.5 G
SODIUM: 22 MG	FIBER: 21.0 G	
CARBOHYDRATES: 91.8 G		SUGAR: 61.0 G

Strawberries for Disease Prevention

Strawberries are a delicious, sweet treat, and they're amazingly healthy, too. Packed with B vitamins, vitamin C, and ellagic acid (an anticancer compound), these rich berries prevent disease and cancer. Shown to help reduce the risk of Alzheimer's disease and lower bad cholesterol, strawberries are essential for any diet in need of an extra boost.

SUNBURN SOOTHER

Vegan, Sweet, Paleo

It's funny to think you could soothe a sunburn with a sweet green smoothie, but it can be done! The hydrating melons are responsible for not only calming skin discomfort, but they also provide electrolytes that promote balance for the body and the mind.

24 OUNCES

1 cup arugula

2 cups cubed and seeded watermelon

2 cups peeled and seeded cantaloupe

½ small lemon, peeled and seeds removed

½ small lime, peeled and seeds removed

½" knob ginger, peeled

2 cups cooled chamomile tea, divided

1. Combine arugula, watermelon, cantaloupe, lemon, lime, ginger, and 1 cup tea in the 24-ounce NutriBullet cup and blend until thoroughly combined.

2. Add remaining 1 cup tea and blend until combined.

3. Consume immediately or store with an airtight lid in the refrigerator for no more than 3–4 hours.

PER 24-OUNCE SERVING		
CALORIES: 226	FAT: 0.9 G	PROTEIN: 5.6 G
SODIUM: 63 MG	FIBER: 6.2 G	
CARBOHYDRATES: 57.2 G		SUGAR: 45.7 G

Melons for Disease Protection

Although most people enjoy these fruits for their hydrating qualities and deliciously sweet flavor, watermelons and cantaloupes are strong warriors in the fight against cancer. Enhancing the immune system with their wealth of B vitamins and vitamin C, these melons have shown to reduce the risks of certain cancers including prostate, ovarian, cervical, oral, and pharyngeal cancers.

AGENT PINEAPPLE AGAINST ARTHRITIS

Vegan, Sweet, Paleo

This vitamin-packed smoothie does a world of good for preventing discomfort associated with everything from common colds to arthritis. Sweet, satisfying, and full of fruits and veggies, this is one smoothie that does it all!

24 OUNCES

1 cup watercress

1 pint blueberries

2 cups peeled, cored, and cubed pineapple

¼" knob ginger, peeled

2 cups cooled chamomile tea, divided

1. Combine watercress, blueberries, pineapple, ginger, and 1 cup tea in the 24-ounce NutriBullet cup and blend until thoroughly combined.

2. Add remaining 1 cup tea and blend until combined.

3. Consume immediately or store with an airtight lid in the refrigerator for no more than 3–4 hours.

PER 24-OUNCE SERVING		
CALORIES: 340	FAT: 0.8 G	PROTEIN: 4.8 G
SODIUM: 22 MG	FIBER: 11.9 G	
CARBOHYDRATES: 87.7 G		SUGAR: 62.1 G

Pineapple Prevention

Did you know that every bite of pineapple has powerful protecting vitamins and enzymes that can drastically reduce the discomfort associated with common ailments? The vitamin C content and the enzyme bromelain are responsible for the major health benefits offered up by this super fruit. Those suffering from asthma, arthritis, angina, and indigestion can find extra relief from indulging in one of nature's most delightfully sweet treats.

FAT-BURNING FUEL

Vegan, Sweet, Paleo

The refreshing combination of watermelon, raspberries, lime, crisp romaine, and calming chamomile will take your life to new heights by improving metabolism and promoting healthy brain function.

24 OUNCES

1 cup romaine lettuce

2 cups cubed and seeded watermelon

1 pint raspberries

½ small lime, peeled and seeds removed

1 cup cooled chamomile tea, divided

1. Combine romaine, watermelon, raspberries, lime, and ½ cup tea in the 24-ounce NutriBullet cup and blend until thoroughly combined.

2. Add remaining ½ cup tea and blend until combined.

3. Consume immediately or store with an airtight lid in the refrigerator for no more than 3–4 hours.

PER 24-OUNCE SERVING		
CALORIES: 237	FAT: 1.5 G	PROTEIN: 5.6 G
SODIUM: 10 MG	FIBER: 19.1 G	
CARBOHYDRATES: 57.9 G		SUGAR: 30.9 G

Vegan, Sweet, Paleo

Reducing aches, pains, soreness, and stiffness can be as easy as blending this delicious fruit, veggie, and herb smoothie that will get you up and moving again!

24 OUNCES

1 cup watercress

2 cups peeled and seeded cantaloupe

1 small cucumber, peeled and sliced

2 tablespoons mint leaves

¼" knob ginger, peeled

1 cup cooled chamomile tea, divided

1. Combine watercress, cantaloupe, cucumber, mint, ginger, and ½ cup tea in the 24-ounce NutriBullet cup and blend until thoroughly combined.

2. Add remaining ½ cup tea and blend until combined.

3. Consume immediately or store with an airtight lid in the refrigerator for no more than 3–4 hours.

PER 24-OUNCE SERVING		
CALORIES: 133	FAT: 0.5 G	PROTEIN: 4.5 G
SODIUM: 69 MG	FIBER: 4.4 G	
CARBOHYDRATES: 31.0 G		SUGAR: 27.4 G

BRIGHT FIGHT AGAINST DISEASE

Vegan, Sweet, Paleo

It's well-known that fruits and veggies signal their potency with their vibrant colors, so imagine the powerful nutrition and antioxidant power of this delightful green blend! In this green smoothie, mangos, strawberries, lemon, sweet romaine, and soothing chamomile combine to fight illness.

24 OUNCES

1 cup romaine lettuce

2 cups peeled, pitted, cubed mango

1 pint strawberries, tops removed

½ small lemon, peeled and seeds removed

2 cups cooled chamomile tea, divided

1. Combine romaine, mangos, strawberries, lemon, and 1 cup tea in the 24-ounce NutriBullet cup and blend until thoroughly combined.

2. Add remaining 1 cup tea and blend until combined.

3. Consume immediately or store with an airtight lid in the refrigerator for no more than 3–4 hours.

PER 24-OUNCE SERVING		
CALORIES: 309	FAT: 1.7 G	PROTEIN: 5.5 G
SODIUM: 12 MG	FIBER: 12.8 G	
CARBOHYDRATES: 76.8 G		SUGAR: 60.5 G

Food Combining for Optimal Benefits

When you're looking for the benefits from fruits and vegetables, how can you possibly decide which is the best? With the varied vitamin and mineral contents in different fruits and vegetables, there isn't a single "best" option. Your best bet would be to include as much nutrition from fruits and vegetables in as wide a variety as possible; the benefits to your immune system, major bodily functions, brain chemistry, and mental processes are innumerable!

SMART START

Vegan, Sweet, Paleo

This smoothie is the perfect way to start your day! Loaded with vitamin- and mineral-rich fruits and greens, this recipe's nutrition and sustaining benefits will last throughout your day.

24 OUNCES

1 cup spinach

1 small apple, peeled, cored, and sliced

1 small Bartlett pear, peeled, cored, and sliced

1 small banana, peeled and sliced

¼" knob ginger, peeled

2 cups cooled chamomile tea, divided

1. Combine spinach, apple, pear, banana, ginger, and 1 cup tea in the 24-ounce NutriBullet cup and blend until thoroughly combined.

2. Add remaining 1 cup tea and blend until combined.

3. Consume immediately or store with an airtight lid in the refrigerator for no more than 3–4 hours.

PER 24–OUNCE SERVING		
CALORIES: 257	FAT: 0.9 G	PROTEIN: 2.9 G
SODIUM: 29 MG	FIBER: 9.7 G	
CARBOHYDRATES: 64.9 G		SUGAR: 40.6 G

VERY GREEN SMOOTHIE

Vegan, Savory, Paleo

This very green smoothie combines a variety of greens for the very best benefits! Spinach, kale, and wheatgrass are packed with vitamins and minerals that work hard to maintain your health.

24 OUNCES

1 cup spinach

2 large kale leaves

1 cup wheatgrass

1 celery stalk

½ small lemon, peeled and seeds removed

1 small garlic clove

1 cup cooled chamomile tea

1. Combine spinach, kale, wheatgrass, celery, lemon, garlic, and tea in the 24-ounce NutriBullet cup and blend until thoroughly combined.

2. Consume immediately or store with an airtight lid in the refrigerator for no more than 3–4 hours.

PER 24-OUNCE SERVING		
CALORIES: 32	FAT: 0.2 G	PROTEIN: 2.4 G
SODIUM: 58 MG	FIBER: 2.3 G	
CARBOHYDRATES: 7.9 G		SUGAR: 2.1 G

ROOT VEGGIE VARIETY

Vegan, Sweet, Paleo

Root vegetables are packed with especially high levels of minerals that promote eye health and offer up protection against a number of cancers. Drink up to promote the best defense against serious illnesses.

24 OUNCES

1 cup romaine lettuce

1 small turnip, peeled and chopped

3 small carrots, peeled, sliced, and tops removed

1 small apple, peeled, cored, and sliced

1 cup water

1. Combine romaine, turnip, carrots, apple, and water in the 24-ounce NutriBullet cup and blend until thoroughly combined.

2. Consume immediately or store with an airtight lid in the refrigerator for no more than 3–4 hours.

PER 24-OUNCE SERVING		
CALORIES: 148	FAT: 0.4 G	PROTEIN: 2.9 G
SODIUM: 155 MG	FIBER: 8.0 G	
CARBOHYDRATES: 36.7 G		SUGAR: 23.3 G

Maximize Your Root Veggie's Potential

One of the many reasons raw food enthusiasts adopt and adhere to the raw food diet is the dramatic drop in vitamins, minerals, and nutrients when produce is heated above a certain temperature. Most people prefer to have their root vegetables steamed, mashed, baked, or roasted, which may taste great, but the scorching heat also scorches a large percentage of the nutrient content. Blending these veggies in a green smoothie is a delicious way to enjoy these superfoods with all of the nutrition nature intended.

COLORFUL COMBO FOR CANCER PREVENTION

Vegan, Sweet, Paleo

Combining for a sweet, down-to-earth flavor, the fruits and vegetables with dark leafy greens and chamomile make for an intoxicating blend for your mind and body's total health.

24 OUNCES

1 cup romaine lettuce

2 cups peeled and seeded cantaloupe

2 small carrots, peeled, sliced, and tops removed

1 cup peeled, cored, and cubed pineapple

1 small beet

1 cup cooled chamomile tea

1. Combine romaine, cantaloupe, carrots, pineapple, beet, and tea in the 24-ounce NutriBullet cup and blend until thoroughly combined.

2. Consume immediately or store with an airtight lid in the refrigerator for no more than 3–4 hours.

PER 24-OUNCE SERVING		
CALORIES: 275	FAT: 0.9 G	PROTEIN: 6.4 G
SODIUM: 189 MG	FIBER: 11.3 G	
CARBOHYDRATES: 67.2 G		SUGAR: 52.3 G

COCOA STRONG SMOOTHIE

Vegan, Sweet, Paleo

Almost every commercially available candy bar consists of refined sugar and manufactured fillers, so be healthy and create your desserts at home. Purchase unsweetened cocoa or 80 percent dark chocolate bars, and you can turn your kitchen into a chocolate shop of homemade delectable delights. By consuming strong cancer-fighting antioxidants, you can extend your life while satisfying your chocolate addiction.

24 OUNCES

2 cups spinach

1 cup frozen mixed berries

1 small banana, peeled and sliced

4 pecan halves

1 tablespoon unsweetened cocoa powder

2 cups unsweetened almond milk

1. Combine spinach, berries, banana, pecans, cocoa powder, and almond milk in the 24-ounce NutriBullet cup and blend until thoroughly combined.

2. Consume immediately or store with an airtight lid in the refrigerator for no more than 3–4 hours.

PER 24-OUNCE SERVING		
CALORIES: 197	FAT: 9.9 G	PROTEIN: 6.7 G
SODIUM: 368 MG	FIBER: 10.5 G	
CARBOHYDRATES: 24.1 G		SUGAR: 10.3 G

SAVOR CANCER PREVENTION

Vegan, Savory, Paleo

Protect yourself by arming your body's defenses with great nutrition that will not only create energy, focus, and total health, but provide strong prevention against serious cancers, too.

24 OUNCES

½ cup romaine lettuce

½ cup spinach

½ cup broccoli spears

½ cup chopped cauliflower

2 small carrots, peeled, sliced, and tops removed

1 celery stalk

1 small garlic clove

1 cup cooled chamomile tea

1. Combine romaine, spinach, broccoli, cauliflower, carrots, celery, garlic, and tea in the 24-ounce NutriBullet cup and blend until thoroughly combined.

2. Consume immediately or store with an airtight lid in the refrigerator for no more than 3–4 hours.

PER 24-OUNCE SERVING		
CALORIES: 87	FAT: 0.4 G	PROTEIN: 4.4 G
SODIUM: 146 MG	FIBER: 6.6 G	
CARBOHYDRATES: 19.2 G		SUGAR: 7.4 G

RED BELLS MAKE HEARTS RING

Vegan, Savory, Paleo

Delicious red peppers star in this simple, savory smoothie. Packed with aromatic red bells peppers, spicy arugula, cooling cucumbers, and crisp celery, this combination is perfect for a filling meal that tastes great and makes for a strong heart.

24 OUNCES

1 cup arugula

1 small red bell pepper, top and seeds removed, ribs intact

2 small cucumbers, peeled and sliced

2 celery stalks

1 cup cooled chamomile tea

1. Combine arugula, red pepper, cucumbers, celery, and tea in the 24-ounce NutriBullet cup and blend until thoroughly combined.

2. Consume immediately or store with an airtight lid in the refrigerator for no more than 3–4 hours.

PER 24-OUNCE SERVING		
CALORIES: 78	FAT: 0.3 G	PROTEIN: 3.7 G
SODIUM: 79 MG	FIBER: 5.3 G	
CARBOHYDRATES: 14.9 G		SUGAR: 9.0 G

ANTIOXIDANT ASSIST

Vegan, Savory, Paleo

No matter how healthy your body may feel, there's always room for some assistance by antioxidants. Warding off illness and preventing degeneration of your body's processes is the main responsibility of these powerful preventers.

24 OUNCES

½ cup arugula

½ cup spinach

½ cup chopped asparagus

½ cup broccoli spears

1 small garlic clove

1 cup cooled chamomile tea

1. Combine arugula, spinach, asparagus, broccoli, garlic, and tea in the 24-ounce NutriBullet cup and blend until thoroughly combined.

2. Consume immediately or store with an airtight lid in the refrigerator for no more than 3–4 hours.

PER 24-OUNCE SERVING		
CALORIES: 39	FAT: 0.2 G	PROTEIN: 3.6 G
SODIUM: 31 MG	FIBER: 3.1 G	
CARBOHYDRATES: 8.0 G		SUGAR: 2.3 G

CAROTENES AGAINST CANCER

Vegan, Sweet, Paleo

The potent healing powers of beta carotene are unleashed in this delicious blend of carrots and sweet potatoes. A satisfying treat for any sweet tooth, you'll be protecting your health with each delicious sip!

24 OUNCES

1 cup romaine lettuce

3 small carrots, peeled, sliced, and tops removed

1 cup peeled and cubed sweet potato

¼" knob ginger, peeled

1 cup cooled chamomile tea

1. Combine romaine, carrots, sweet potato, ginger, and tea in the 24-ounce NutriBullet cup and blend until thoroughly combined.

2. Consume immediately or store with an airtight lid in the refrigerator for no more than 3–4 hours.

PER 24-OUNCE SERVING		
CALORIES: 250	FAT: 0.6 G	PROTEIN: 6.0 G
SODIUM: 180 MG	FIBER: 11.8 G	
CARBOHYDRATES: 57.9 G		SUGAR: 20.6 G

CAULIFLOWER TO THE RESCUE

Vegan, Sweet, Paleo

This smoothie lets cauliflower make a grand entrance by showcasing its grand capabilities and health benefits for anyone in need of brain and heart health! Including this powerful veggie in this delicious smoothie makes a great recipe even greater!

24 OUNCES

1 cup romaine lettuce

1 cup chopped cauliflower

2 small carrots, peeled, sliced, and tops removed

1 small apple, peeled, cored, and sliced

1 cup cooled chamomile tea

1. Combine romaine, cauliflower, carrots, apple, and tea in the 24-ounce NutriBullet cup and blend until thoroughly combined.

2. Consume immediately or store with an airtight lid in the refrigerator for no more than 3–4 hours.

PER 24-OUNCE SERVING		
CALORIES: 139 G	FAT: 0.5 G	PROTEIN: 3.9 G
SODIUM: 106 MG	FIBER: 7.6 G	
CARBOHYDRATES: 33.8 G		SUGAR: 20.7 G

Ever Heard of Allicin?

The amazing powers of cauliflower are not enjoyed enough in the standard American diet. Offering important nutrition that satisfies daily dietary needs, this stark white veggie is packing a powerful secret weapon, too. Cauliflower provides allicin, an important compound that actually reduces the risk of stroke and heart disease while detoxifying the blood and liver. With abilities like that, this veggie is a must-have in any disease-preventing diet.

PEAR SPLENDOR

Vegan, Sweet, Paleo

Pears give this smoothie its unique sweetness and taste, while the banana adds a sweet, smooth texture. Packed with vitamins and nutrients, this smoothie is a sweet and tasty fiber-filled delight!

24 OUNCES

1 cup spinach

2 small Bartlett pears, peeled, cored, and sliced

1 small banana, peeled and sliced

1 cup unsweetened almond milk, divided

1. Combine spinach, pears, banana, and ½ cup almond milk in the 24-ounce NutriBullet cup and blend until smooth.

2. Add remaining almond milk and blend until combined.

3. Consume immediately or store with an airtight lid in the refrigerator for no more than 3–4 hours.

PER 24-OUNCE SERVING		
CALORIES: 316	FAT: 2.8 G	PROTEIN: 4.1 G
SODIUM: 187 MG	FIBER: 12.7 G	
CARBOHYDRATES: 69.8 G		SUGAR: 41.9 G

The Power of Copper

A little-known fact about the pear is that just 1 serving contains a powerful amount of copper. A strong and very important mineral, copper works wonders in fighting the process of free-radical damage to cells. Not only does this mean a pear can help you fight off cancer and disease, but the aesthetic effects of antiaging are pretty attractive, too!

CALMING CUCUMBER

Vegan, Savory, Paleo

Even though a cucumber is mostly water (and fiber), it is far more than a tasty, hydrating, and filling snack option. These green veggies are great foods to eat if you want healthier skin. A clear complexion is an aesthetic benefit of consuming cucumbers. By consuming 1 serving of cucumbers per day, you'll not only fulfill a full serving of veggies and stave off hunger, but you'll have clear, hydrated skin!

24 OUNCES

1 cup romaine lettuce

2 small cucumbers, peeled and sliced

¼ cup mint leaves

1 cup water, divided

1. Combine romaine, cucumbers, mint, and ½ cup water in the 24-ounce NutriBullet cup and blend until thoroughly combined.

2. Add remaining ½ cup water and blend until combined.

3. Consume immediately or store with an airtight lid in the refrigerator for no more than 3–4 hours.

PER 24-OUNCE SERVING		
CALORIES: 48	FAT: 0.2 G	PROTEIN: 2.7 G
SODIUM: 19 MG	FIBER: 3.7 G	
CARBOHYDRATES: 9.3 G		SUGAR: 4.9 G

COOL CUCUMBER MELON

Sweet

The mix of romaine, cucumbers, honeydew, and mint in this recipe combine beautifully to develop one of the most crisp, refreshing smoothies you'll taste.

24 OUNCES

1 cup romaine lettuce

1 sprig mint leaves

3 small cucumbers, peeled and sliced

½ small honeydew melon, peeled, seeds removed

½ cup kefir, divided

1. Combine romaine and mint leaves followed by the cucumbers, melon, and ¼ cup kefir in the 24-ounce NutriBullet cup and blend until thoroughly combined.

2. Add remaining ¼ cup kefir and blend until combined.

3. Consume immediately or store with an airtight lid in the refrigerator for no more than 3–4 hours.

PER 24-OUNCE SERVING		
CALORIES: 248	FAT: 4.4 G	PROTEIN: 9.1 G
SODIUM: 126 MG	FIBER: 8.4 G	
CARBOHYDRATES: 45.8 G		SUGAR: 36.2 G

CHOCOLATEY DREAM

Vegan, Sweet, Paleo

Ahhhh, chocolate! It's pretty difficult to find someone who doesn't like chocolate, and this smoothie has the perfect blend of ingredients to satisfy any chocolate craving. In addition, chocolate has been determined to be beneficial in the daily diet! Don't take this as a go-ahead to dive into that huge bag of M&M's, though. Powdered, unprocessed cocoa is the chocolate shown to provide the most benefits. Although the candy bar alternative may seem more gratifying, the sugar content, trans fats, and milk products may be the reason it hasn't yet been labeled a superfood.

24 OUNCES

1 cup watercress

2 tablespoons raw cacao powder

2 small bananas, peeled and sliced

2 cups unsweetened almond milk, divided

1. Combine the watercress and cacao powder followed by the bananas and 1 cup almond milk in the 24-ounce NutriBullet cup and blend until thoroughly combined.

2. Add remaining 1 cup almond milk and blend until combined.

3. Consume immediately or store with an airtight lid in the refrigerator for no more than 3–4 hours.

PER 24-OUNCE SERVING		
CALORIES: 290	FAT: 6.6 G	PROTEIN: 7.4 G
SODIUM: 343 MG	FIBER: 8.6 G	
CARBOHYDRATES: 53.8 G		SUGAR: 24.8 G

CHAPTER 7

SMOOTHIES THAT ENERGIZE

Smoothies are healthy, but green smoothies . . . well, they are insanely good for you! Greens, especially the dark leafy ones found in the recipes in this chapter, purify the blood, fight infection, build the immune system, boost brain function, reduce the damage of free radicals (molecules created by stress), and provide energy through folate (a type of B complex vitamin).

The recipes in this chapter will show you how you can use your NutriBullet to create green smoothies that will keep you going all day long—and each contains a handful or two of leafy greens like romaine lettuce, watercress, dandelion greens, baby greens, spinach, and more! You can substitute a favorite leaf for all the greens in these recipes. But do yourself a favor: If you've never tried some of the greens listed here, be adventurous. It is easy to get in a habit of only including your favorite greens, but try a mix. Not only does the nutritional benefit of each green vary, but the taste and texture differ also, offering limitless combinations when blended with other ingredients. Buying a bag of mixed greens is helpful to use on those extremely busy or even lazy weeks. No "thinking" needed. Throw a couple handfuls in with your favorite fruit/veggie/liquid combination and life is good.

CARROT TOP OF THE MORNING TO YOU

Vegan, Sweet, Paleo

Rich in beta carotene, this smoothie blends romaine lettuce with tasty carrots and apples to give you a sweet start that can help you stay focused, provide lasting energy, and maintain the health of your eyes and metabolism.

24 OUNCES

1 cup romaine lettuce

2 small carrots, peeled, sliced, and tops removed

1 small apple, peeled, cored, and sliced

1 cup water

1. Combine lettuce, carrots, and apple in the 24-ounce NutriBullet cup and blend until thoroughly combined.

2. Add water and blend until combined.

3. Consume immediately or store with an airtight lid in the refrigerator for no more than 3–4 hours.

PER 24-OUNCE SERVING		
CALORIES: 111	FAT: 0.3 G	PROTEIN: 1.9 G
SODIUM: 81 MG	FIBER: 5.5 G	
CARBOHYDRATES: 28.0 G		SUGAR: 18.6 G

Carrots Can Save the Day!

With the ability to protect your body from cancer, heart attacks, premature aging, and poor vision, this vegetable is a must-have in your daily diet. Its rich orange color is the telltale sign that it is rich in beta carotene (vitamin A), but it's also packed with B vitamins, vitamin K, and potassium. Talk about a multitasker!

MANGO TANGO

Vegan, Sweet, Paleo

The fruits in this smoothie offer an incredibly sweet and smooth texture that evens out the bitterness of the dandelion greens nicely. This fruity blend will leave you energized and ready to conquer the most hectic morning!

24 OUNCES

½ cup dandelion greens

½ cup iceberg lettuce

1 small mango, peeled and pitted

½ cup peeled, cored, and cubed pineapple

½ small orange, peeled and seeds removed

½ cup water, divided

1. Combine dandelion greens, iceberg, mango, pineapple, orange, and ¼ cup water in the 24-ounce NutriBullet cup and blend until thoroughly combined.

2. Add remaining water and blend until combined.

3. Consume immediately or store with an airtight lid in the refrigerator for no more than 3–4 hours.

PER 24-OUNCE SERVING		
CALORIES: 279	FAT: 1.2 G	PROTEIN: 4.7 G
SODIUM: 29 MG	FIBER: 9.0 G	
CARBOHYDRATES: 70.2 G		SUGAR: 59.3 G

GRAPEFRUIT AND CUCUMBER ENERGY

Vegan, Sweet, Paleo

The grapefruit and cucumber combine in this smoothie to offer a refreshing zing to your morning with vitamins and nutrients that will wake you up and keep you feeling fresh throughout the day!

24 OUNCES

1 cup baby greens

1 small grapefruit, peeled and seeds removed

1 small cucumber, peeled and sliced

¼ cup water, divided

1. Combine greens, grapefruit, cucumber, and 2 tablespoons water and blend until thoroughly combined.

2. Add remaining 2 tablespoons water and blend until combined.

3. Consume immediately or store with an airtight lid in the refrigerator for no more than 3–4 hours.

PER 24-OUNCE SERVING		
CALORIES: 146	FAT: 0.2 G	PROTEIN: 4.0 G
SODIUM: 37 MG	FIBER: 6.0 G	
CARBOHYDRATES: 37.2 G		SUGAR: 30.1 G

Why Grapefruit Is Great

Although the grapefruit is known for being rich in vitamin C, this citrus fruit has not only been used for building immunity but also for treating symptoms of illness. The next time you start feeling feverish, the best thing to take may just be a healthy helping of grapefruit, which would make this smoothie the perfect option!

LUSCIOUS LEMON-LIME

Sweet

The tartness of lemons and limes is cooled off with crisp romaine and sweet agave nectar. The kefir gives a creamy texture with protein and essential vitamins. The ingredients combine in a delicious smoothie that will make you feel awake and energized.

24 OUNCES

1 cup romaine lettuce

2 small lemons, peeled and seeds removed

2 small limes, peeled and seeds removed

½ cup kefir

1 tablespoon agave nectar

1. Combine romaine, lemons, limes, and kefir in the 24-ounce NutriBullet cup and blend until thoroughly combined.

2. Add agave nectar and blend until combined.

3. Consume immediately or store with an airtight lid in the refrigerator for no more than 3–4 hours.

PER 24-OUNCE SERVING		
CALORIES: 221	FAT: 4.3 G	PROTEIN: 6.8 G
SODIUM: 69 MG	FIBER: 10.5 G	
CARBOHYDRATES: 50.0 G		SUGAR: 26.7 G

Balance Your Body

Not only do lemons and limes have the acidity and tang to make you pucker up, but they are incredibly healthy, too. Those same small, sour fruits that can bring a tear to your eye actually promote a balanced alkaline level in your body.

APPLE PEACH

Vegan, Sweet, Paleo

Apples, peaches, and almond milk create a sweet, smooth blend that complements the green watercress. If you're looking for a healthy snack, skip the processed sweets and energy drinks and opt for this quick and easy blend that will give you sustainable energy for the rest of your day.

24 OUNCES

1 cup watercress

3 small peaches, pitted and peeled

2 small apples, peeled, cored, and sliced

2 cups unsweetened almond milk, divided

1. Combine watercress, peaches, apples, and 1 cup almond milk in the 24-ounce NutriBullet cup and blend until thoroughly combined.

2. Add remaining 1 cup almond milk and blend until combined.

3. Consume immediately or store with an airtight lid in the refrigerator for no more than 3–4 hours.

PER 24-OUNCE SERVING		
CALORIES: 341	FAT: 5.8 G	PROTEIN: 7.0 G
SODIUM: 333 MG	FIBER: 9.5 G	
CARBOHYDRATES: 71.3 G		SUGAR: 59.5 G

TRAIL MIX SMOOTHIE

Vegan, Sweet, Paleo

Ingest your trail mix in liquid form before your hike with this delicious smoothie. It will yield lasting energy while you maneuver your way through the forest, rocks, and water—or as you move through a long day at the office.

24 OUNCES

2 cups spinach

¼ cup unsweetened coconut flakes

1 medium apple, peeled, cored, and sliced

¼ cup fresh goji berries

1 tablespoon unsweetened cocoa powder

4 pecan halves

1 tablespoon raw sunflower seeds

2 Medjool dates, pitted and diced

2 cups unsweetened almond milk

1. Combine spinach, coconut, apple, goji berries, cocoa powder, pecans, sunflower seeds, dates, and almond milk in the 24-ounce NutriBullet cup and blend until thoroughly combined.

2. Consume immediately or store with an airtight lid in the refrigerator for no more than 3–4 hours.

PER 24-OUNCE SERVING		
CALORIES: 576	FAT: 23.8 G	PROTEIN: 13.2 G
SODIUM: 448 MG	FIBER: 24.1 G	
CARBOHYDRATES: 92.6 G		SUGAR: 54.0 G

TOMATILLO MARY SMOOTHIE

Vegan, Savory, Paleo

The tomatillos in this Bloody Mary alternative are loaded with nutritional benefits that help increase your energy levels. In addition, the jalapeño provides a little kick in the middle of the afternoon as well as vitamins A and C, phenols, flavonoids, and capsaicinoids that help the body fight inflammation.

24 OUNCES

2 cups spinach

1 tablespoon cilantro

3 tomatillos, husked and cored

1 small green onion, trimmed and chopped

½ small lime, peeled and seeds removed

1 small cucumber, peeled and sliced

½ small jalapeño, seeds removed

Pinch of sea salt

2 cups water

1. Combine spinach, cilantro, tomatillos, onion, lime, cucumber, jalapeño, salt, and water in the 24-ounce NutriBullet cup and blend until thoroughly combined.

2. Consume immediately or store with an airtight lid in the refrigerator for no more than 3–4 hours.

PER 24-OUNCE SERVING		
CALORIES: 76	FAT: 0.9 G	PROTEIN: 4.0 G
SODIUM: 359 MG	FIBER: 5.7 G	
CARBOHYDRATES: 15.9 G		SUGAR: 7.4 G

FENNEL-CUCUMBER SMOOTHIE

Vegan, Savory, Paleo

Pairing fennel, which is high in vitamin C, and spinach, which is high in iron, will help maximize your body's absorption of iron. If you are suffering from anemia, this smoothie will aid in transporting oxygen to your tissues, which will result in higher energy levels.

24 OUNCES

1 cup spinach

1 small fennel bulb, including fronds (strip these from the tough, yet edible, stalks)

½ small cucumber, peeled and sliced

1 celery stalk, with leaves

1 medium carrot, peeled, sliced, and top removed

Pinch of sea salt

2 cups water

1. Combine spinach, fennel, cucumber, celery, carrot, salt, and water in the 24-ounce NutriBullet cup and blend until thoroughly combined.

2. Consume immediately or store with an airtight lid in the refrigerator for no more than 3–4 hours.

PER 24-OUNCE SERVING		
CALORIES: 113	FAT: 0.9 G	PROTEIN: 5.0 G
SODIUM: 519 MG	FIBER: 10.5 G	
CARBOHYDRATES: 25.9 G		SUGAR: 13.3 G

BERRY PRETTY SMOOTHIE

Vegan, Sweet, Paleo

Blueberries, blackberries, strawberries, and raspberries are super-foods disguised as sweet treats. These fat-burning fruits are low in calories, packed with antioxidants that promote weight loss, and supply quick energy that allows you to burn fat fast. They are also rich in magnesium, one of the most important minerals in promoting energy regulation.

24 OUNCES

2 cups spinach

2 small apples, peeled, cored, and sliced

1 cup frozen mixed berries

½ small lemon, peeled and seeds removed

1 cup water

1 cup unsweetened almond milk

1. Combine spinach, apples, berries, lemon, water, and almond milk in the 24-ounce NutriBullet cup and blend until thoroughly combined.

2. Consume immediately or store with an airtight lid in the refrigerator for no more than 3–4 hours.

PER 24-OUNCE SERVING		
CALORIES: 236	FAT: 3.0 G	PROTEIN: 4.6 G
SODIUM: 216 MG	FIBER: 10.5 G	
CARBOHYDRATES: 53.3 G		SUGAR: 35.5 G

ENERGETIC ARTICHOKE SMOOTHIE

Vegan, Sweet, Paleo

Although artichokes are most commonly used in salads and appetizers, raw artichokes make for a tasty addition to green smoothies such as this one and are high in carbohydrates, making them an instant source of energy. Artichokes also pack a protective punch against colon cancer, inflammation, and bone loss.

24 OUNCES

2 cups spinach

4 small artichoke hearts

1 small tart apple, peeled, cored, and sliced

1 medium carrot, peeled, sliced, and top removed

2 cups cooled green tea

1. Combine spinach, artichokes, apple, carrot, and tea in the 24-ounce NutriBullet cup and blend until thoroughly combined.

2. Consume immediately or store with an airtight lid in the refrigerator for no more than 3–4 hours.

PER 24-OUNCE SERVING		
CALORIES: 200	FAT: 0.3 G	PROTEIN: 10.5 G
SODIUM: 365 MG	FIBER: 24.5 G	
CARBOHYDRATES: 48.8 G		SUGAR: 20.0 G

CHAPTER 8

SMOOTHIES FOR PRE– AND POSTWORKOUT

You may be surprised to hear that green smoothies can help to both optimize your workouts and help you cool down afterward, but it's true! The smoothies found in this chapter—like the Metabolism Max Out, Banana Berry Boost, Protein Packer, Rapid Recovery, and more!—contain complex carbohydrates, protein, and healthy fats in combination with essential vitamins, minerals, and phytochemicals from nutrient-dense superfoods. Supporting the entire body's intricate systems and parts, these delicious recipes revitalize, rejuvenate, and protect with quality nutrition that will help you transform your health, your body, and your life.

CARROT COMMANDO

Vegan, Sweet, Paleo

Carrots, spinach, and apples combine for a delightfully sweet and filling smoothie. They provide loads of important vitamins and minerals needed for optimal functioning of all those body systems designed to make you move and help you move faster.

24 OUNCES

1 cup spinach

4 small carrots, peeled, sliced, and tops removed

2 small apples, peeled, cored, and sliced

1 cup water

1. Combine spinach, carrots, apples, and water in the 24-ounce NutriBullet cup and blend until thoroughly combined.

2. Consume immediately or store with an airtight lid in the refrigerator for no more than 3–4 hours.

PER 24-OUNCE SERVING		
CALORIES: 214	FAT: 0.5 G	PROTEIN: 3.4 G
SODIUM: 170 MG	FIBER: 9.7 G	
CARBOHYDRATES: 53.9 G		SUGAR: 36.3 G

Carrots for Flushing an Athlete's Fat Stores
Among the many capabilities of carrots, one little-known function is its assistance to the liver's cleansing power. Carrots aid the liver's cleansing process by keeping it squeaky clean and helping to more efficiently move excess bile and fat stores out of the body. With this important vegetable helping this star organ, you could suffer from less digestive disorders and have better regularity and an overall "lighter" feeling from its toxin- and fat-flushing abilities and diuretic effect.

RAPID RECOVERY

Savory

Tasty and powerful, this recipe's ingredients provide powerful protein from intense vitamin- and mineral-rich veggies. The addition of the lemon and garlic benefit your body by promoting a healthy metabolic level for more efficient fat burning.

24 OUNCES

1 cup watercress

1 cup broccoli spears

1 celery stalk

½ small lemon, peeled and seeds removed

1 small garlic clove

1 cup nonfat Greek-style yogurt

1. Combine watercress, broccoli, celery, lemon, garlic, and yogurt in the 24-ounce NutriBullet cup and blend until thoroughly combined.

2. Consume immediately or store with an airtight lid in the refrigerator for no more than 3–4 hours.

PER 24–OUNCE SERVING		
CALORIES: 214	FAT: 0.7 G	PROTEIN: 25.0 G
SODIUM: 157 MG	FIBER: 4.7 G	
CARBOHYDRATES: 30.0 G		SUGAR: 20.4 G

Yogurt for Rapid Recovery

We know protein delivers recovery aid to our muscles, but what is the best type to deliver maximum benefits and reap the most rewards? Chicken, beef, pork, and fish all come with saturated fats and aren't suitable for vegetarian athletes. If you're not interested in a protein shake of the powdered variety, turn to Greek-style yogurt! It has twice as much protein (20 grams), has fewer carbs (9 grams or less), and half the sodium of regular yogurt.

BROCCOLI BLASTOFF

Vegan, Savory, Paleo

Broccoli and kale add a great dose of protein in this smoothie. If you're looking for even more protein, there is the delightful option of protein powders in a variety of flavors that would blend nicely with savory smoothies such as this.

24 OUNCES

2 large kale leaves

1 cup broccoli spears

½ small red bell pepper, top and seeds removed, ribs intact

2 celery stalks

1 small green onion, trimmed and chopped

1 small garlic clove

1 cup water

1. Combine kale, broccoli, red pepper, celery, onion, garlic, and water in the 24-ounce NutriBullet cup and blend until thoroughly combined.

2. Consume immediately or store with an airtight lid in the refrigerator for no more than 3–4 hours.

PER 24-OUNCE SERVING		
CALORIES: 59	FAT: 0.2 G	PROTEIN: 3.9 G
SODIUM: 105 MG	FIBER: 4.8 G	
CARBOHYDRATES: 12.4 G		SUGAR: 4.4 G

ZOOM WITH ZUCCHINI

Vegan, Savory, Paleo

The vibrant veggies and cayenne pepper in this recipe make for a fat-burning, calorie-zapping smoothie that will fill you up and fire your engines!

24 OUNCES

1 cup spinach

1 small zucchini, peeled and sliced

1 small tomato, sliced

2 celery stalks

1 small green onion, trimmed and chopped

2 small garlic cloves

⅛ teaspoon cayenne pepper

2 cups water, divided

1. Combine spinach, zucchini, tomato, celery, onion, garlic, cayenne, and 1 cup water in the 24-ounce NutriBullet cup and blend until thoroughly combined.

2. Add remaining 1 cup water and blend until combined.

3. Consume immediately or store with an airtight lid in the refrigerator for no more than 3–4 hours.

PER 24-OUNCE SERVING		
CALORIES: 76	FAT: 1.0 G	PROTEIN: 5.1 G
SODIUM: 126 MG	FIBER: 5.4 G	
CARBOHYDRATES: 15.5 G		SUGAR: 8.7 G

SWEET SPINACH SPINNER

Vegan, Sweet, Paleo

This sweet spin on vitamin-rich spinach makes a delightful treat you can enjoy before or after an exercise session. The low glycemic index of the ingredients makes a sustainable energy-powering blend of vitamins, minerals, and phytochemicals that will help you perform without the energy crash of caffeinated energy drinks.

24 OUNCES

1 cup spinach

4 small apples, peeled, cored, and sliced

¼" knob ginger, peeled

1 cup water

1. Combine spinach, apples, ginger, and water in the 24-ounce NutriBullet cup and blend until thoroughly combined.

2. Consume immediately or store with an airtight lid in the refrigerator for no more than 3–4 hours.

PER 24-OUNCE SERVING		
CALORIES: 259	FAT: 0.3 G	PROTEIN: 2.3 G
SODIUM: 32 MG	FIBER: 7.5 G	
CARBOHYDRATES: 68.6 G		SUGAR: 53.5 G

POWERFUL PARSNIPS

Vegan, Sweet, Paleo

Packed with vitamin C, parsnips make a tasty ingredient in this surprisingly sweet smoothie. Packed with important minerals for energy and stamina, root veggies are a great way to maximize your smoothie's potency potential.

24 OUNCES

1 cup watercress

1 small parsnip, peeled

3 small carrots, peeled, sliced, and tops removed

1 cup water

1. Combine watercress, parsnip, carrots, and water in the 24-ounce NutriBullet cup and blend until thoroughly combined.

2. Consume immediately or store with an airtight lid in the refrigerator for no more than 3–4 hours.

PER 24–OUNCE SERVING		
CALORIES: 163	FAT: 0.5 G	PROTEIN: 3.8 G
SODIUM: 138 MG	FIBER: 10.9 G	
CARBOHYDRATES: 38.8 G		SUGAR: 13.6 G

KILLER KALE KICKOFF

Vegan, Savory, Paleo

Packed with an abundance of vitamin K, a fat-soluble compound, kale is a healthy way to get a good amount of this vitamin. This smoothie is a one-stop shop that delivers important vitamins and minerals that promote focus and sustainable energy.

24 OUNCES

2 large kale leaves

4 small carrots, peeled, sliced, and tops removed

1 small cucumber, peeled and sliced

2 small green onions, trimmed and chopped

2 small garlic cloves

1 cup water

1. Combine kale, carrots, cucumber, onions, garlic, and water in the 24-ounce NutriBullet cup and blend until thoroughly combined.

2. Consume immediately or store with an airtight lid in the refrigerator for no more than 3–4 hours.

PER 24-OUNCE SERVING		
CALORIES: 112	FAT: 0.4 G	PROTEIN: 3.5 G
SODIUM: 153 MG	FIBER: 7.2 G	
CARBOHYDRATES: 25.6 G		SUGAR: 12.0 G

PROTEIN PACKER

Sweet

The tasteful, creamy combination of sweet fruits and almonds blends beautifully with the crisp watercress for a protein-packed delight you're sure to enjoy after a strenuous workout.

24 OUNCES

¼ cup almonds

¾ cup water

1 cup watercress

1 small apple, peeled, cored, and sliced

1 small banana, peeled and sliced

1 cup Greek-style yogurt, divided

1. Combine almonds and water in the 24-ounce NutriBullet cup and blend until emulsified and no almond bits remain.

2. Add watercress, apple, banana, and ½ cup yogurt and blend until thoroughly combined.

3. Add remaining ½ cup yogurt and blend until combined.

4. Consume immediately or store with an airtight lid in the refrigerator for no more than 3–4 hours.

PER 24–OUNCE SERVING		
CALORIES: 578	FAT: 29.0 G	PROTEIN: 30.0 G
SODIUM: 102 MG	FIBER: 8.3 G	
CARBOHYDRATES: 56.7 G		SUGAR: 36.6 G

COLLIDE WITH COLLARDS

Vegan, Savory, Paleo

Refreshing and nutritious, this blend delivers powerful vitamins and minerals that work as hard as you do. To fuel your body's powerful energy requirements and replenish your muscles' stores, green veggies are your best bet for complete, balanced nutrition!

24 OUNCES

1 cup collard greens

1 cup chopped cauliflower

1 cup broccoli spears

1 small carrot, peeled, sliced, and top removed

1 cup water

1. Combine collards, cauliflower, broccoli, carrot, and water in the 24-ounce NutriBullet cup and blend until thoroughly combined.

2. Consume immediately or store with an airtight lid in the refrigerator for no more than 3–4 hours.

PER 24-OUNCE SERVING		
CALORIES: 87	FAT: 0.4 G	PROTEIN: 6.2 G
SODIUM: 111 MG	FIBER: 7.4 G	
CARBOHYDRATES: 18.1 G		SUGAR: 6.1 G

POPEYE'S FAVORITE

Vegan, Savory, Paleo

Popeye had the right idea, and it showed in his powerful abilities. This recipe is filled with iron, vitamin K, folate, and fiber, and will have you feeling strong like Popeye!

24 OUNCES

1 cup spinach

1 large kale leaf

1 cup broccoli spears

3 small apples, peeled, cored, and sliced

1 cup water

1. Combine spinach, kale, broccoli, apples, and water in the 24-ounce NutriBullet cup and blend until thoroughly combined.

2. Consume immediately or store with an airtight lid in the refrigerator for no more than 3–4 hours.

PER 24-OUNCE SERVING		
CALORIES: 227	FAT: 0.4 G	PROTEIN: 4.6 G
SODIUM: 62 MG	FIBER: 8.3 G	
CARBOHYDRATES: 57.9 G		SUGAR: 41.7 G

Greens for All

When you were a kid, Popeye was one amazing example of what could happen if you ate your spinach! How many times did your parents reference Popeye when trying to get you to eat your spinach? And how often do you reference strength when trying to get your kids to eat greens now? Spinach is packed with vitamins A, B, C, E, and K as well as iron, phosphorous, and fiber. With all of that nutrition delivered in each serving, spinach should be in every athlete's daily diet!

METABOLISM MAX OUT

Vegan, Sweet, Paleo

Vitamin C plays an important part in fighting illness, promoting your body's ability to function properly in every aspect, and optimizing metabolism for a fat-burning effect like no other.

24 OUNCES

1 cup watercress

2 cups peeled, cored, and cubed pineapple

1 small white grapefruit, peeled and seeds removed

3 small tangerines, peeled

1 small lemon, peeled and seeds removed

½ cup cooled green tea

1. Combine watercress, pineapple, grapefruit, tangerines, lemon, and tea in the 24-ounce NutriBullet cup and blend until thoroughly combined.

2. Consume immediately or store with an airtight lid in the refrigerator for no more than 3–4 hours.

PER 24-OUNCE SERVING		
CALORIES: 433	FAT: 0.8 G	PROTEIN: 7.6 G
SODIUM: 22 MG	FIBER: 14.9 G	
CARBOHYDRATES: 112.1 G		SUGAR: 86.1 G

BANANA BERRY BOOST

Sweet

You can't beat the taste of smooth bananas and sweet berries blended with creamy yogurt! There's no better follow up to a satisfying workout than a dose of sweet fruits blended with powerful protein to optimize your muscles' recovery.

24 OUNCES

1 cup watercress

2 small bananas, peeled and sliced

2 cups dried goji berries

1 cup Greek-style yogurt, divided

1. Combine watercress, bananas, goji berries, and ½ cup yogurt in the 24-ounce NutriBullet cup and blend until thoroughly combined.

2. Add remaining ½ cup yogurt and blend until combined.

3. Consume immediately or store with an airtight lid in the refrigerator for no more than 3–4 hours.

PER 24-OUNCE SERVING		
CALORIES: 1,159	FAT: 11.9 G	PROTEIN: 55.6 G
SODIUM: 695 MG	FIBER: 101.4 G	
CARBOHYDRATES: 247.7 G		SUGAR: 65.9 G

The Goji Berry

Goji berries provide excellent health benefits for everything from cancer prevention to eye health. Although research has shown the nutrients and phytochemicals in berries are responsible for preventing serious illnesses and diseases, the goji berry's specific effects are still under review. Including these sweet jewels makes for one delicious smoothie that will not only satisfy your sweet tooth but also make your body a flu-fighting machine.

VIVACIOUS VITAMIN C

Vegan, Sweet, Paleo

Eating a balanced diet of vibrant fruits, vegetables, and leafy greens can ensure you're providing for your health and your athletic ability.

24 OUNCES

1 cup watercress

½ small pineapple, peeled, cored, and cubed

3 small oranges, peeled and seeds removed

1 small lemon, peeled and seeds removed

1 cup strawberries, tops removed

1 cup water, divided

1. Combine watercress, pineapple, oranges, lemon, strawberries, and ½ cup water in the 24-ounce NutriBullet cup and blend until thoroughly combined.

2. Add remaining ½ cup water and blend until combined.

3. Consume immediately or store with an airtight lid in the refrigerator for no more than 3–4 hours.

PER 24-OUNCE SERVING		
CALORIES: 317	FAT: 0.7 G	PROTEIN: 6.4 G
SODIUM: 26 MG	FIBER: 14.9 G	
CARBOHYDRATES: 81.6 G		SUGAR: 58.7 G

Vitamins and Minerals for Proactive Health

How important is vitamin C to an athlete? When was the last time you saw a top-performing athlete take first place hacking and heaving all the way to the finish line? Never! If you're going to keep your body in top shape, ready for anything, sound nutrition isn't the only thing requiring attention. In order to get the biggest bang for your buck out of performance nutrition, load up on vibrant fruits and veggies that do double duty.

SWEET POTATO SMOOTHIE

Vegan, Sweet, Paleo

Even though being an avid athlete means focusing on the healthiest foods that provide ideal nutrition calorie for calorie, cravings for sweet treats creep up every once in a while. Calm those cravings with combinations like this that satisfy with sound nutrition!

24 OUNCES

½ cup walnuts

1½ cups water, divided

1 cup spinach

1 small sweet potato, peeled and cubed

1 teaspoon pumpkin pie spice

1. Combine walnuts and 1 cup water in the 24-ounce NutriBullet cup and blend until emulsified and no walnut bits remain.

2. Add spinach, sweet potato, pumpkin pie spice, and remaining ½ cup water and blend until combined.

3. Consume immediately or store with an airtight lid in the refrigerator for no more than 3–4 hours.

PER 24-OUNCE SERVING		
CALORIES: 465	FAT: 40.3 G	PROTEIN: 12.2 G
SODIUM: 58 MG	FIBER: 6.9 G	
CARBOHYDRATES: 22.7 G		SUGAR: 6.2 G

Walnuts for Athletic Performance

In just ¼ cup of walnuts you can find almost 100 percent of your daily value of omega-3s with the richness of monounsaturated fats. Not only a tasty, protein-packed morsel, the walnut helps athletes perform at their best by improving circulation and heart health, controlling blood pressure, providing essential amino acids, and acting as a powerful antioxidant.

CACAO CRAZINESS

Vegan, Sweet, Paleo

Chocolate cravings can end in guilty consumption of sugar- and fat-laden candy that leads to the need for more exercise. Satisfy those cravings with pure cacao in a smoothie like this, and candy cravings will be a thing of the past.

24 OUNCES

¼ cup almonds

1½ cups water, divided

1 cup watercress

2 tablespoons raw cacao powder

2 small bananas, peeled and sliced

2 small apples, peeled, cored, and sliced

1. Combine almonds and 1 cup water in the 24-ounce NutriBullet cup and blend until emulsified and no almond bits remain.

2. Add watercress, cacao, bananas, apples, and remaining ½ cup water and blend until combined.

3. Consume immediately or store with an airtight lid in the refrigerator for no more than 3–4 hours.

PER 24–OUNCE SERVING		
CALORIES: 554	FAT: 18.9 G	PROTEIN: 12.9 G
SODIUM: 30 MG	FIBER: 14.6 G	
CARBOHYDRATES: 93.5 G		SUGAR: 53.1 G

Sweet Antioxidant Protection

When in need of powerful antioxidants that provide and protect, reach no further than a heaping helping of raw cacao. The plant that actually delivers the cocoa we're familiar with, cacao is known as a superfood for providing an abundance of antioxidants. Protect your body and the hard work you've put into making it an efficient machine by adding raw cacao in sweet or savory smoothies for an extra hit of health!

RUNNER'S DELIGHT

Sweet

Any endurance runner feels amped before and pumped following a run. After all that hard work, you're definitely entitled to enjoy a sweet treat. Instead of undoing all that hard work with empty calories, indulge in the sweet taste of citrus with all its added benefits!

24 OUNCES

1 cup watercress

3 small oranges, peeled and seeds removed

1 cup strawberries, tops removed

1 cup raspberries

1 cup Greek-style yogurt, divided

1. Combine watercress, oranges, berries, and ½ cup yogurt in the 24-ounce NutriBullet cup and blend until thoroughly combined.

2. Add remaining ½ cup yogurt and blend until combined.

3. Consume immediately or store with an airtight lid in the refrigerator for no more than 3–4 hours.

PER 24-OUNCE SERVING		
CALORIES: 464	FAT: 12.4 G	PROTEIN: 26.5 G
SODIUM: 95 MG	FIBER: 18.0 G	
CARBOHYDRATES: 69.2 G		SUGAR: 48.6 G

A BIKER'S BEST FRIEND

Vegan, Sweet, Paleo

Nothing keeps sustained energy up like slow-releasing carbohydrates. Root vegetables are the best friends of any distance cyclist on a mission for better times and better health!

24 OUNCES

Enough water to cover yams, plus 1 cup

2 small yams, peeled and cubed

1 cup spinach

2 small apples, peeled, cored, and sliced

2 small carrots, peeled, sliced, and tops removed

1. Fill a medium saucepan halfway with water. Add yams and bring to a boil. Boil for about 10 minutes or until yams are tender. Remove yams from heat, strain, and set aside to cool, about 15 minutes.

2. Combine yams, spinach, apples, carrots, and 1 cup water in the 24-ounce NutriBullet cup and blend until thoroughly combined.

3. Consume immediately or store with an airtight lid in the refrigerator for no more than 3–4 hours.

PER 24-OUNCE SERVING		
CALORIES: 370	FAT: 0.5 G	PROTEIN: 5.0 G
SODIUM: 114 MG	FIBER: 13.5 G	
CARBOHYDRATES: 91.1 G		SUGAR: 32.4 G

Sweet

Despite the fact that you are surrounded by water while swimming, you can come out feeling dehydrated and in need of a boost of energy. A refreshing combination of pineapple, lemon, and cooling cucumbers can deliver exactly what your mind and body need.

24 OUNCES

1 cup iceberg lettuce

2 cups peeled, cored, and cubed pineapple

2 small cucumbers, peeled and sliced

½ small lemon, peeled and seeds removed

1 cup Greek-style yogurt, divided

1. Combine iceberg, pineapple, cucumbers, lemon, and ½ cup yogurt in the 24-ounce NutriBullet cup and blend until thoroughly combined.

2. Add remaining ½ cup yogurt and blend until combined.

3. Consume immediately or store with an airtight lid in the refrigerator for no more than 3–4 hours.

PER 24–OUNCE SERVING		
CALORIES: 434	FAT: 11.8 G	PROTEIN: 25.1 G
SODIUM: 94 MG	FIBER: 8.3 G	
CARBOHYDRATES: 63.7 G		SUGAR: 47.9 G

Sweet

Yoga, hot or not, can be a powerful workout. Replenish your body and refresh your senses with this sweet blend of melons, citrus, and berries. A definite "Yum!" to follow your "Ohm!"

24 OUNCES

1 cup watercress

½ small honeydew, rind and seeds removed

2 small tangerines, peeled and seeds removed

1 small cucumber, peeled and sliced

1 cup Greek-style yogurt, divided

1. Combine watercress, honeydew, tangerines, cucumber, and ½ cup yogurt in the 24-ounce NutriBullet cup and blend until thoroughly combined.

2. Add remaining ½ cup yogurt and blend until combined.

3. Consume immediately or store with an airtight lid in the refrigerator for no more than 3–4 hours.

PER 24-OUNCE SERVING		
CALORIES: 523	FAT: 12.2 G	PROTEIN: 26.6 G
SODIUM: 201 MG	FIBER: 8.6 G	
CARBOHYDRATES: 85.1 G		SUGAR: 73.8 G

OH MY! OMEGAS

Vegan, Sweet, Paleo

In this tasty recipe, omega-3s are plentiful without the need for salmon or rich meats. If salmon isn't your favorite food, consider smoothies that contain flaxseed for your daily value of omegas.

24 OUNCES

1 cup watercress

½ small cantaloupe, peeled and seeds removed

1 small banana, peeled and sliced

1 small orange, peeled and seeds removed

1 cup raspberries

1 tablespoon flaxseed

1 cup water

1. Combine watercress, cantaloupe, banana, orange, raspberries, flaxseed, and water in the 24-ounce NutriBullet cup and blend until thoroughly combined.

2. Consume immediately or store with an airtight lid in the refrigerator for no more than 3–4 hours.

PER 24-OUNCE SERVING		
CALORIES: 329	FAT: 5.2 G	PROTEIN: 8.0 G
SODIUM: 62 MG	FIBER: 17.9 G	
CARBOHYDRATES: 70.4 G		SUGAR: 44.3 G

Flaxseed for Omega-3s!

Everybody needs omegas! Although many athletes include meats in their diets, some vegetarian and vegan athletes need to turn to alternatives to fulfill their omega needs. Flaxseed provides an amazing amount of omegas that are comparable to rich meats (that are also high in undesirable fat content) and fish. Flaxseed makes a mildly nutty addition to your favorite smoothie blends.

FABULOUS FRUCTOSE

Vegan, Sweet, Paleo

The combination of citrus fruits in this smoothie will give you the nutrients you need after a great workout.

24 OUNCES

1 cup romaine lettuce

½ small pineapple, peeled, cored, and cubed

½ small red grapefruit, peeled and seeds removed

1 small tangerine, peeled and seeds removed

½ small lemon, peeled and seeds removed

½ small lime, peeled and seeds removed

½ cup water

1. Combine romaine, pineapple, grapefruit, tangerine, lemon, lime, and water in the 24-ounce NutriBullet cup and blend until thoroughly combined.

2. Consume immediately or store with an airtight lid in the refrigerator for no more than 3–4 hours.

PER 24-OUNCE SERVING		
CALORIES: 246	FAT: 0.5 G	PROTEIN: 4.3 G
SODIUM: 10 MG	FIBER: 9.6 G	
CARBOHYDRATES: 65.0 G		SUGAR: 47.0 G

Fructose: The Smart Sugar

Fructose, the natural sugar found in fruit, is the healthiest version of sugar because it's an all-natural, nonprocessed version of the table sugars and artificial sweeteners commonly used. As an athlete, fruit is an important source for vitamins and minerals because it can satisfy your cravings for sweets without the unhealthy crash associated with processed sugar or the possible health risks associated with artificial sweeteners.

WONDER WATERMELON

Sweet

Watermelon's super powers don't end with its amazing hydrating effects, which make it one of the top go-to summer fruits. This delicious smoothie with the hidden taste of romaine will make a veggie eater of your pickiest eater!

24 OUNCES

1 cup romaine lettuce

2 cups cubed and seeded watermelon

2 small bananas, peeled and sliced

½ cup Greek-style yogurt

1 cup ice

1. Combine romaine, watermelon, bananas, and yogurt in the 24-ounce NutriBullet cup and blend until thoroughly combined.

2. Add ice and blend until combined.

3. Consume immediately or store with an airtight lid in the refrigerator for no more than 3–4 hours.

PER 24-OUNCE SERVING		
CALORIES: 385	FAT: 6.5 G	PROTEIN: 14.9 G
SODIUM: 48 MG	FIBER: 7.5 G	
CARBOHYDRATES: 75.2 G		SUGAR: 48.7 G

WHAT THE HILL SMOOTHIE

Vegan, Sweet, Paleo

Whether you are hitting the open road or killing a spin class, cycling can burn some serious calories. Adding coconut oil to a preworkout smoothie can give you longer-lasting energy. Because it is a "good" fat and fat burns slower than carbohydrates, it is exactly what you need to help power through and get up and down those hills.

24 OUNCES

2 cups mixed greens

2 cups frozen strawberries

1 small banana, peeled and sliced

¼ cup cashews

2 teaspoons coconut oil

1 cup unsweetened almond milk

1 cup water

1. Combine greens, strawberries, banana, cashews, coconut oil, almond milk, and water in the 24-ounce NutriBullet cup and blend until thoroughly combined.

2. Consume immediately or store with an airtight lid in the refrigerator for no more than 3–4 hours.

PER 24-OUNCE SERVING		
CALORIES: 693	FAT: 41.7 G	PROTEIN: 14.9 G
SODIUM: 250 MG	FIBER: 11.9 G	
CARBOHYDRATES: 75.7 G		SUGAR: 29.4 G

CHAPTER 9

SMOOTHIES FOR BETTER BRAIN FUNCTION

Hate forgetting things? Feel like you are absentminded a little too often? Need something to help get your brain back in the game? Well, the green smoothies found in this chapter are designed to get your brain back on track with rich sources of vitamins and minerals that stimulate and rejuvenate brain functions. With NutriBlast smoothies packed full of vitamins such as Bs, C, and E; minerals such as iron, magnesium, potassium, manganese, zinc, and calcium; and of course protective and preventative nutrients like omegas, antioxidants, anti-inflammatories, proteins, fats, and carbohydrates, you'll have your focus back in no time.

MENTAL MAKEOVER

Vegan, Savory, Paleo

In addition to being a rich source of iron and folate (which actually aids in iron absorption), the spinach in this smoothie holds a wealth of vitamins (A, B, C, and K) that provide cancer-fighting power against liver, ovarian, colon, and prostate cancers. By including just 1 cup of this powerful veggie in your daily diet (raw), you can satisfy over 180 percent of your daily value for vitamin K and over 50 percent of your vitamin A intake!

24 OUNCES

1 cup spinach

2 small cucumbers, peeled and sliced

2 celery stalks

1 small tomato, sliced

1 cup cooled chamomile tea

1. Combine spinach, cucumbers, celery, tomato, and tea in the 24-ounce NutriBullet cup and blend until thoroughly combined.

2. Consume immediately or store with an airtight lid in the refrigerator for no more than 3–4 hours.

PER 24-OUNCE SERVING		
CALORIES: 73	FAT: 0.4 G	PROTEIN: 4.1 G
SODIUM: 99 MG	FIBER: 5.2 G	
CARBOHYDRATES: 14.3 G		SUGAR: 8.0 G

MEMORY MAINTAINER

Vegan, Savory, Paleo

Protecting your brain was never this delicious! The vitamins, minerals, and antioxidants that promote optimal functioning of your mental processes also prevent the brain's deterioration from illness and disease. This is one smoothie you won't forget!

24 OUNCES

1 cup romaine lettuce

½ cup broccoli spears

½ cup chopped cauliflower

1 small tomato, sliced

1 small garlic clove

1 cup water

1. Combine romaine, broccoli, cauliflower, tomato, garlic, and water in the 24-ounce NutriBullet cup and blend until thoroughly combined.

2. Consume immediately or store with an airtight lid in the refrigerator for no more than 3–4 hours.

PER 24-OUNCE SERVING		
CALORIES: 55	FAT: 0.4 G	PROTEIN: 3.9 G
SODIUM: 47 MG	FIBER: 4.4 G	
CARBOHYDRATES: 11.8 G		SUGAR: 4.8 G

BLUEBERRY BURST

Sweet

Not only does the delicious blend of blueberries and bananas taste great, but this combination makes for an amazingly nutritional treat! The rich potassium, magnesium, B_6, and electrolyte stores of the bananas add to the vitamin C, saponins, and powerful antioxidants of the blueberries for a delicious way to promote heart health, energy, and immune-boosting power, but most of all mental clarity and focus!

24 OUNCES

1 cup watercress

2 pints blueberries

2 small bananas, peeled and sliced

1 cup blueberry kefir

1 cup ice

1. Combine watercress, blueberries, bananas, and kefir in the 24-ounce NutriBullet cup container and blend until thoroughly combined.

2. Add ice and blend until smooth.

3. Consume immediately or store with an airtight lid in the refrigerator for no more than 3–4 hours.

PER 24-OUNCE SERVING		
CALORIES: 669	FAT: 3.6 G	PROTEIN: 13.4 G
SODIUM: 190 MG	FIBER: 20.6 G	
CARBOHYDRATES: 158.4 G		SUGAR: 105.7 G

A BERRY GREAT MORNING

Vegan, Sweet

The vitamins and phytochemicals that burst from the raspberries and blueberries found in this green smoothie help fight off the cancers, carcinogens, and mental health risks that you'd rather steer clear of!

24 OUNCES

2 cups mixed baby greens

1 pint raspberries

1 pint blueberries

1 small banana, peeled and sliced

¼ cup vanilla soymilk

1. Combine greens, berries, and banana and blend thoroughly.

2. Add soymilk and blend until combined.

3. Consume immediately or store with an airtight lid in the refrigerator for no more than 3–4 hours.

PER 24-OUNCE SERVING		
CALORIES: 410	FAT: 2.8 G	PROTEIN: 8.8 G
SODIUM: 98 MG	FIBER: 26.8 G	
CARBOHYDRATES: 101.3 G		SUGAR: 54.9 G

Vegan, Sweet, Paleo

Booming with the strong flavors of pineapple, orange, grapefruit, lemon, and lime, this sweet and tart smoothie will liven your senses while providing you with a boost in physical and mental health.

24 OUNCES

2 large kale leaves

1 cup peeled, cored, and cubed pineapple

1 small orange, peeled and seeds removed

½ small grapefruit, peeled and seeds removed

½ small lemon, peeled and seeds removed

½ small lime, peeled and seeds removed

1. Combine kale, pineapple, orange, grapefruit, lemon, and lime in the 24-ounce NutriBullet cup and blend until thoroughly combined.

2. Consume immediately or store with an airtight lid in the refrigerator for no more than 3–4 hours.

PER 24-OUNCE SERVING		
CALORIES: 210	FAT: 0.3 G	PROTEIN: 3.8 G
SODIUM: 2 MG	FIBER: 8.7 G	
CARBOHYDRATES: 55.7 G		SUGAR: 40.6 G

VERY IMPORTANT VITAMIN C

Vegan, Sweet, Paleo

Not only does vitamin C make for an important addition to your diet for its strong immunity-building power, but this vitamin also provides optimal brain functioning, which means better mental clarity, improved focus, and an overall feeling of awareness.

24 OUNCES

1 cup watercress

2 small tangerines, peeled and seeds removed

½ small grapefruit, peeled and seeds removed

½ small pineapple, peeled, cored, and cubed

½ small cantaloupe, peeled and seeds removed

1 cup cooled red raspberry tea

1. Combine watercress, tangerines, grapefruit, pineapple, and cantaloupe in the 24-ounce NutriBullet cup and blend until thoroughly combined.

2. Add tea and blend until combined.

3. Consume immediately or store with an airtight lid in the refrigerator for no more than 3–4 hours.

PER 24-OUNCE SERVING		
CALORIES: 340	FAT: 0.8 G	PROTEIN: 6.4 G
SODIUM: 55 MG	FIBER: 10.4 G	
CARBOHYDRATES: 86.2 G		SUGAR: 70.6 G

THE SLUMP BUMPER

Vegan, Sweet, Paleo

Packed with an assortment of vitamins and minerals, an obvious sign from their intense red color, cherries help mental functions like memory. Cherries also improve mental clarity and promote focus and attention.

24 OUNCES

1 cup spinach

2 small Bartlett pears, peeled, cored, and sliced

1 cup pitted cherries

1 small banana, peeled and sliced

1 cup unsweetened almond milk

1. Combine spinach, pears, cherries, banana, and almond milk in the 24-ounce NutriBullet cup and blend until thoroughly combined.

2. Consume immediately or store with an airtight lid in the refrigerator for no more than 3–4 hours.

PER 24-OUNCE SERVING		
CALORIES: 413	FAT: 3.0 G	PROTEIN: 5.8 G
SODIUM: 187 MG	FIBER: 15.9 G	
CARBOHYDRATES: 94.4 G		SUGAR: 61.7 G

ROMAINE TO THE RESCUE!

Vegan, Savory, Paleo

Crisp romaine, broccoli, carrots, garlic, and ginger combine in this recipe to make for one satisfying, savory smoothie that will promote health for your eyes, digestion, muscle repair, and mental clarity.

24 OUNCES

2 cups romaine lettuce

½ cup broccoli spears

2 small carrots, peeled, sliced, and tops removed

1 small garlic clove

½" knob ginger, peeled

1 cup water

1. Combine romaine, broccoli, carrots, garlic, ginger, and water in the 24-ounce NutriBullet cup and blend until thoroughly combined.

2. Consume immediately or store with an airtight lid in the refrigerator for no more than 3–4 hours.

PER 24-OUNCE SERVING		
CALORIES: 75	FAT: 0.3 G	PROTEIN: 3.6 G
SODIUM: 100 MG	FIBER: 6.0 G	
CARBOHYDRATES: 16.9 G		SUGAR: 6.7 G

PEARS WITH A TART TWIST

Vegan, Sweet, Paleo

Providing an amazing percentage of essential vitamins and minerals needed for the optimal functioning of your mind and body, this smoothie is a sweet, tart, and smart way to pep up your day!

24 OUNCES

4 cups romaine lettuce

2 small Bartlett pears, peeled, cored, and sliced

1 small banana, peeled and sliced

6 tablespoons lemon juice

1 cup water

1. Combine romaine, pears, banana, lemon juice, and water in the 24-ounce NutriBullet cup and blend until thoroughly combined.

2. Consume immediately or store with an airtight lid in the refrigerator for no more than 3–4 hours.

PER 24-OUNCE SERVING		
CALORIES: 331	FAT: 1.6 G	PROTEIN: 4.9 G
SODIUM: 28 MG	FIBER: 16.3 G	
CARBOHYDRATES: 81.2 G		SUGAR: 46.4 G

GREEN SWEET CITRUS

Vegan, Sweet, Paleo

This recipe is a wonderfully refreshing option for any time your body and mind may need a boost. The mildly peppery taste of watercress combines with the citrus flavors to develop a light and refreshing vitamin-packed treat.

24 OUNCES

1 cup watercress

1 small grapefruit, peeled and seeds removed

2 small oranges, peeled and seeds removed

½" knob ginger, peeled

½ small lemon, peeled and seeds removed

½ cup water

1. Combine watercress, grapefruit, oranges, ginger, lemon, and water in the 24-ounce NutriBullet cup and blend until thoroughly combined.

2. Consume immediately or store with an airtight lid in the refrigerator for no more than 3–4 hours.

PER 24-OUNCE SERVING		
CALORIES: 165	FAT: 0.2 G	PROTEIN: 4.2 G
SODIUM: 31 MG	FIBER: 7.8 G	
CARBOHYDRATES: 42.1 G		SUGAR: 32.7 G

WATERCRESS BERRY

Vegan, Sweet, Paleo

Blend these delightfully fresh fruits with the refreshing taste of watercress, and the only overwhelming feeling you'll encounter is pure pleasure. Your mouth and body will benefit from the vitamins and minerals—and your mind will thank you, too!

24 OUNCES

1 cup watercress

2 small oranges, peeled and seeds removed

1 cup strawberries, tops removed

1 cup blueberries

½ cup unsweetened CoconutMilk

1. Combine watercress, oranges, strawberries, blueberries, and CoconutMilk in the 24-ounce NutriBullet cup and blend until thoroughly combined.

2. Consume immediately or store with an airtight lid in the refrigerator for no more than 3–4 hours.

PER 24-OUNCE SERVING		
CALORIES: 245	FAT: 2.7 G	PROTEIN: 4.7 G
SODIUM: 32 MG	FIBER: 11.2 G	
CARBOHYDRATES: 55.5 G		SUGAR: 39.8 G

The Importance of Antioxidants

Illnesses, cancers, and diseases all have their own individual origins and causes, but the danger and contribution to these debilitating conditions by free radicals and oxidative processes is well-known. The antioxidants in fruits and vegetables combat these types of sickness. By including berries, greens, and a colorful assortment of fruits and vegetables in your diet, you're increasing your chances of living a longer, healthier life.

PEAS, PLEASE!

Vegan, Sweet, Paleo

Providing more than 50 percent of the recommended daily amount of vitamin K in 1 cup, and packed with B vitamins, vitamin C, iron, zinc, manganese, and protein, peas are a great choice for a regular addition to your diet. Promoting brain health, bone strength, heart health, and disease-fighting protection, these sweet green morsels are worth their weight in health!

24 OUNCES

1 cup spinach

1 cup sweet peas

2 small carrots, peeled, sliced, and tops removed

1 small apple, peeled, cored, and sliced

1 cup cooled green tea

½ cup ice

1. Combine spinach, peas, carrots, apple, and tea in the 24-ounce NutriBullet cup and blend until thoroughly combined.

2. Add ice and blend until combined.

3. Consume immediately or store with an airtight lid in the refrigerator for no more than 3–4 hours.

PER 24-OUNCE SERVING		
CALORIES: 229	FAT: 1.1 G	PROTEIN: 10.0 G
SODIUM: 101 MG	FIBER: 12.6 G	
CARBOHYDRATES: 49.0 G		SUGAR: 26.4 G

CHAPTER 10

SMOOTHIES FOR TOTAL HEALTH AND DISEASE PREVENTION

Fresh, green produce is good for your body for many reasons related to the healing vitamins and minerals that are introduced to your system. Each piece of produce has its own makeup of vitamins and minerals that help different organs and body functions do what they were meant to do. Drinking green smoothies like The Pollinator Smoothie, Pear Prevention, and the Breathe Easy Smoothie found in this chapter allows you to combine a variety of these healthy ingredients in a quick, portable meal. Avocados lend creaminess to smoothies as well as being a great preventative ingredient in the fight against oral cancer. Carrots add a natural sweetness while giving your body a dose of beta carotene, converted into vitamin A to support a healthy immune system and good eye health. So drink up for good taste and to prevent health problems.

POMEGRANATE PREVENTER

Vegan, Sweet, Paleo

Packed with vitamins and minerals that promote health and fight illness, blending these delicious fruits and vegetables is a tasty way to maintain great health.

24 OUNCES

1 cup iceberg lettuce

2 cups pomegranate arils

1 small orange, peeled and seeds removed

1 small banana, peeled and sliced

¾ cup water, divided

1. Combine iceberg, pomegranate, orange, banana, and ½ cup water in the 24-ounce NutriBullet cup and blend until thoroughly combined.

2. Add remaining ¼ cup water and blend until combined.

3. Consume immediately or store with an airtight lid in the refrigerator for no more than 3–4 hours.

PER 24-OUNCE SERVING		
CALORIES: 429	FAT: 4.3 G	PROTEIN: 8.1 G
SODIUM: 25 MG	FIBER: 19.6 G	
CARBOHYDRATES: 100.0 G		SUGAR: 70.5 G

CANTALOUPE FOR CANCER PREVENTION

Vegan, Sweet, Paleo

The vibrant color of cantaloupe is from the abundant levels of beta carotene, known for providing health benefits. Not only a sweet treat, this smoothie provides a wide variety of vitamins and minerals that work hard in preventing illness and disease.

24 OUNCES

1 cup watercress

½ small cantaloupe, peeled and seeds removed

1 small apple, peeled, cored, and sliced

1 small banana, peeled and sliced

¼" knob ginger, peeled

¾ cup water, divided

1. Combine watercress, cantaloupe, apple, banana, ginger, and ½ cup water in the 24-ounce NutriBullet cup and blend until thoroughly combined.

2. Add remaining ¼ cup water and blend until combined.

3. Consume immediately or store with an airtight lid in the refrigerator for no more than 3–4 hours.

PER 24–OUNCE SERVING		
CALORIES: 229	FAT: 0.6 G	PROTEIN: 4.1 G
SODIUM: 56 MG	FIBER: 6.5 G	
CARBOHYDRATES: 58.4 G		SUGAR: 43.1 G

Beta Carotene's Fight Against Cancer

Among the many benefits beta carotene offers, one of the major functions of this strong antioxidant is to combat free radicals from the environment, certain foods, and unhealthy lifestyles. Free radicals can cause abnormal growth in cells, which can lead to dangerous illnesses like cancer. Studies have shown that diets rich in carotenes promote proper cell growth, thereby reducing the chances of cancers and disease.

BLACKBERRY WATERCRESS SMOOTHIE

Sweet

Delicious blackberries are made even more tasty with the addition of lemon and ginger in this recipe. This smoothie packs a healthy dose of much-needed vitamins and minerals, and is rich and satisfying with the addition of protein-packed yogurt.

24 OUNCES

1 cup watercress

2 pints blackberries

1 small banana, peeled and sliced

½ small lemon, peeled and seeds removed

½" knob ginger, peeled

½ cup Greek-style yogurt

1. Combine watercress, blackberries, banana, lemon, ginger, and yogurt in the 24-ounce NutriBullet cup and blend until thoroughly combined.

2. Consume immediately or store with an airtight lid in the refrigerator for no more than 3–4 hours.

PER 24-OUNCE SERVING		
CALORIES: 455	FAT: 7.9 G	PROTEIN: 20.5 G
SODIUM: 59 MG	FIBER: 34.2 G	
CARBOHYDRATES: 86.3 G		SUGAR: 45.8 G

BREATHE EASY SMOOTHIE

Vegan, Sweet, Paleo

Rich, plump blackberries are not just a tasty treat; they are also packed with a variety of vitamins and minerals that can aid in overall health. Specifically, the magnesium content in blackberries helps relax the muscles and thin the mucus most commonly associated with breathing difficulties.

24 OUNCES

2 cups spinach

1 cup frozen blackberries

1 cup frozen pitted cherries

8 almonds

1½ cups unsweetened almond milk

1. Combine spinach, blackberries, cherries, almonds, and almond milk in the 24-ounce NutriBullet cup and blend until thoroughly combined.

2. Consume immediately or store with an airtight lid in the refrigerator for no more than 3–4 hours.

PER 24-OUNCE SERVING		
CALORIES: 286	FAT: 10.0 G	PROTEIN: 8.6 G
SODIUM: 289 MG	FIBER: 12.5 G	
CARBOHYDRATES: 45.1 G		SUGAR: 30.8 G

Sweet

Vitamins K and C, beta carotene, potassium, folate, and protein are rich in this delicious smoothie. A one-stop shop for many of your fruit and vegetable servings, this delicious recipe satisfies your sweet tooth and dietary needs.

24 OUNCES

1 cup romaine lettuce

1 cup peeled, cored, and cubed pineapple

1 pint strawberries, tops removed

1 small banana, peeled and sliced

½ cup Greek-style yogurt

1. Combine romaine, pineapple, strawberries, banana, and yogurt in the 24-ounce NutriBullet cup and blend until thoroughly combined.

2. Consume immediately or store with an airtight lid in the refrigerator for no more than 3–4 hours.

PER 24-OUNCE SERVING		
CALORIES: 378	FAT: 6.7 G	PROTEIN: 14.8 G
SODIUM: 47 MG	FIBER: 11.7 G	
CARBOHYDRATES: 73.0 G		SUGAR: 47.8 G

BERRIES AND BANANAS FOR BONE HEALTH

Sweet

The crisp taste of iceberg lettuce is beautifully balanced with the addition of citrus, blackberries, bananas, and yogurt for a flavor combination that will make you enjoy eating better for your health.

24 OUNCES

1 cup iceberg lettuce

1 pint blackberries

1 cup peeled, cored, and cubed pineapple

2 small bananas, peeled and sliced

½ cup Greek-style yogurt

1. Combine iceberg, blackberries, pineapple, bananas, and yogurt in the 24-ounce NutriBullet cup and blend until thoroughly combined.

2. Consume immediately or store with an airtight lid in the refrigerator for no more than 3–4 hours.

PER 24-OUNCE SERVING		
CALORIES: 499	FAT: 7.2 G	PROTEIN: 17.9 G
SODIUM: 50 MG	FIBER: 23.5 G	
CARBOHYDRATES: 101.7 G		SUGAR: 60.7 G

Magnesium for Bone Health

The magnesium in blackberries can do amazing things for respiratory relief, but it can also help create stronger bones because it plays an important role in the absorption of calcium. Diets deficient in magnesium have also shown to prevent the body's proper use of estrogen, which can spell disaster for many of the body's cancer-fighting abilities.

A GRAPE WAY TO BONE HEALTH

Vegan, Sweet, Paleo

You may never have heard of anthocyanin and proanthocyanidin, but these two amazing compounds are extremely important in promoting strong bones and optimizing bone health. Anthocyanins and proanthocyanidins are compounds found in cells, and their duty is to ensure the bone structure is stabilized and to promote the collagen-building process that is absolutely imperative for strong bones. The two main foods packed with these strong compounds are deep-red and purple grapes and blueberries.

24 OUNCES

1 cup watercress

2 cups red seedless grapes

2 small Bartlett pears, peeled, cored, and sliced

1 small banana, peeled and sliced

½ cup water

1. Combine watercress, grapes, pears, banana, and water in the 24-ounce NutriBullet cup and blend until thoroughly combined.

2. Consume immediately or store with an airtight lid in the refrigerator for no more than 3–4 hours.

PER 24-OUNCE SERVING		
CALORIES: 491	FAT: 1.3 G	PROTEIN: 5.2 G
SODIUM: 27 MG	FIBER: 14.9 G	
CARBOHYDRATES: 123.8 G		SUGAR: 88.6 G

VITAMIN C CANCER PREVENTION

Vegan, Sweet, Paleo

This vitamin C–packed recipe is a delicious blend of grapefruit, pineapple, and orange, intensified by the addition of ginger and spinach, which is rich in vitamin K and iron. Not only is vitamin C well-known for illness prevention, but it works absolute wonders in many areas for promoting optimal health. In addition to being a strong supporter of bone health by improving the collagen-building process, building and retaining quality muscle, and improving the efficiency of blood vessels, it actually aids in the body's absorption of iron. Common mineral deficiencies can be reversed by including an abundance of vitamin C with your daily intake of iron-rich foods.

24 OUNCES

1 cup spinach

1 small grapefruit, peeled and seeds removed

1 cup peeled, cored, and cubed pineapple

1 small orange, peeled and seeds removed

½" knob ginger, peeled

¾ cup water, divided

1. Combine spinach, grapefruit, pineapple, orange, ginger, and ½ cup water in the 24-ounce NutriBullet cup and blend until thoroughly combined.

2. Add remaining ¼ cup water and blend until smooth.

3. Consume immediately or store with an airtight lid in the refrigerator for no more than 3–4 hours.

PER 24-OUNCE SERVING		
CALORIES: 261	FAT: 0.4 G	PROTEIN: 5.2 G
SODIUM: 31 MG	FIBER: 9.7 G	
CARBOHYDRATES: 66.5 G		SUGAR: 53.3 G

A COOL BLEND FOR BLOOD SUGARS

Sweet

Maintaining a diet that optimizes sugar levels to ensure diabetic health is easy with this delicious blend. The combination of ingredients makes a refreshing treat that will keep you going when you need a boost.

24 OUNCES

1 cup watercress

1 celery stalk

1 small cucumber, peeled and sliced

2 small Bartlett pears, peeled, cored, and sliced

2 tablespoons mint leaves

¾ cup Greek-style yogurt, divided

1. Combine watercress, celery, cucumber, pears, mint, and ½ cup yogurt in the 24-ounce NutriBullet cup and blend until thoroughly combined.

2. Add remaining ¼ cup yogurt and blend until combined.

3. Consume immediately or store with an airtight lid in the refrigerator for no more than 3–4 hours.

PER 24-OUNCE SERVING		
CALORIES: 382	FAT: 8.7 G	PROTEIN: 18.7 G
SODIUM: 111 MG	FIBER: 11.6 G	
CARBOHYDRATES: 58.0 G		SUGAR: 39.1 G

CHERRY VANILLA RESPIRATORY RELIEF

Vegan, Sweet, Paleo

Move over, ice cream! This delicious smoothie will have you wondering, "Where's the greens?" Although the overpowering flavors of cherry and vanilla take center stage, the vitamin and mineral content of all of the ingredients (including the spinach) will do your body a world of good.

24 OUNCES

1 cup spinach

2 cups pitted cherries

1 small apple, peeled, cored, and sliced

Pulp of 1 vanilla bean

½" knob ginger, peeled

1 cup water

1. Combine spinach, cherries, apple, vanilla, ginger, and water in the 24-ounce NutriBullet cup and blend until thoroughly combined.

2. Consume immediately or store with an airtight lid in the refrigerator for no more than 3–4 hours.

PER 24-OUNCE SERVING		
CALORIES: 283	FAT: 1.0 G	PROTEIN: 4.5 G
SODIUM: 32 MG	FIBER: 9.9 G	
CARBOHYDRATES: 71.4 G		SUGAR: 56.0 G

The Breathing Benefit of Cherries

The abundant phytochemical content in cherries is what lends a hand to your breathing. Phytochemicals make an impact on inflammation everywhere in the body. Commonly suggested for patients suffering from inflammation of joints, cherries can also assist in reducing the inflammation of airways and respiratory-related muscles. By including these powerful antioxidant- and vitamin-rich berries in your diet, you'll fight off illnesses that make breathing difficult and promote a more efficient respiratory process.

Sweet

If your diet and lifestyle leave you feeling in need of refreshment and vitality, this smoothie is for you. Hydrating melon and citrus combine with rich greens to provide a revitalizing lift.

24 OUNCES

1 cup watercress

2 cups cubed and seeded watermelon

1 cup peeled, cored, and cubed pineapple

¾ cup kefir

1. Combine watercress, watermelon, pineapple, and kefir in the 24-ounce NutriBullet cup and blend until thoroughly combined.

2. Consume immediately or store with an airtight lid in the refrigerator for no more than 3–4 hours.

PER 24-OUNCE SERVING		
CALORIES: 297	FAT: 6.4 G	PROTEIN: 9.5 G
SODIUM: 110 MG	FIBER: 6.0 G	
CARBOHYDRATES: 56.3 G		SUGAR: 44.2 G

APPLE CELERY FOR HYDRATION

Vegan, Sweet, Paleo

The fruits and greens in this smoothie provide natural sugars and carbohydrates, and celery regulates water levels.

24 OUNCES

1 cup romaine lettuce

3 small Granny Smith apples, peeled, cored, and sliced

2 celery stalks

¼" knob ginger, peeled

1¼ cups water, divided

1. Combine romaine, apples, celery, ginger, and 1 cup water in the 24-ounce NutriBullet cup and blend until thoroughly combined.

2. Add remaining ¼ cup water and blend until combined.

3. Consume immediately or store with an airtight lid in the refrigerator for no more than 3–4 hours.

PER 24–OUNCE SERVING		
CALORIES: 209	FAT: 0.4 G	PROTEIN: 2.2 G
SODIUM: 78 MG	FIBER: 7.4 G	
CARBOHYDRATES: 54.6 G		SUGAR: 41.6 G

The Body's Need for Water

Cravings, fatigue, lack of focus, and derailed bodily functions can all result from not getting adequate water. The minimum recommended water intake is eight 8-ounce glasses of water daily, but those who exercise require even more. In addition to the water added while blending, the fruits and vegetable in this smoothie deliver one tasty way to increase your hydration.

"PEA" IS FOR PREVENTION

Vegan, Sweet, Paleo

Sweetening this smoothie with sweet green peas makes a delightful treat. This tasty blend of watercress, cucumbers, and peas delivers a refreshing and filling snack with amazing health benefits from all of the rich ingredients.

24 OUNCES

1 cup watercress

2 small cucumbers, peeled and sliced

1 cup petite sweet green peas

1¼ cups water, divided

1. Combine watercress, cucumbers, peas, and 1 cup water in the 24-ounce NutriBullet cup and blend until thoroughly combined.

2. Add remaining ¼ cup water and blend until combined.

3. Consume immediately or store with an airtight lid in the refrigerator for no more than 3–4 hours.

PER 24-OUNCE SERVING		
CALORIES: 157	FAT: 0.5 G	PROTEIN: 10.5 G
SODIUM: 37 MG	FIBER: 9.8 G	
CARBOHYDRATES: 28.2 G		SUGAR: 12.7 G

The Power of a Pea

Adding just 1 cup of this sweet veggie to your daily diet will provide more than 50 percent of your daily recommended intake of vitamin K, along with vitamins B and C, manganese, fiber, and protein. This results in stronger bones; heightened disease prevention; efficient metabolism of carbohydrates, fats, and proteins; improved cardiac health; and more energy.

GEAR UP WITH GARLIC

Vegan, Savory, Paleo

This savory smoothie makes a delicious meal replacement for an invigorating breakfast, satisfying lunch, or delightful dinner. The strong flavors of spinach and garlic combine with the cucumber, tomato, and celery for a taste sensation to savor.

24 OUNCES

1 cup spinach

1 small cucumber, peeled and sliced

1 celery stalk

1 small tomato, sliced

2 small garlic cloves

1¼ cups water, divided

1. Combine spinach, cucumber, celery, tomato, garlic, and 1 cup water in the 24-ounce NutriBullet cup and blend until thoroughly combined.

2. Add remaining ¼ cup water and blend until combined.

3. Consume immediately or store with an airtight lid in the refrigerator for no more than 3–4 hours.

PER 24-OUNCE SERVING		
CALORIES: 54	FAT: 0.3 G	PROTEIN: 3.3 G
SODIUM: 74 MG	FIBER: 3.6 G	
CARBOHYDRATES: 11.2 G		SUGAR: 5.3 G

Garlic Prep for Optimal Benefits

Cooking garlic for as little as 60 seconds has shown to cause it to lose some of its anticancer properties. Packed with an abundance of vitamins, minerals, and nutrients that work hard to fight cancer and heart disease, prevent bacterial and viral infections, improve iron metabolism, control blood pressure, and act as an anti-inflammatory, garlic's abilities can be optimized by crushing or chopping it and preparing it without heat.

A PEPPERY WAY TO PROMOTE HEALTH

Vegan, Savory, Paleo

Spicy arugula and red pepper join forces with crisp celery and spicy garlic for a spicy treat with a bite in this smoothie rich in vitamins and antioxidants.

24 OUNCES

1 cup arugula

2 celery stalks

½ small red bell pepper, top and seeds removed, ribs intact

1 small garlic clove

1½ cups water, divided

1. Combine arugula, celery, red pepper, garlic, and ¾ cup water in the 24-ounce NutriBullet cup and blend until thoroughly combined.

2. Add remaining ¾ cup water and blend until combined.

3. Consume immediately or store with an airtight lid in the refrigerator for no more than 3–4 hours.

PER 24-OUNCE SERVING		
CALORIES: 32	FAT: 0.2 G	PROTEIN: 1.6 G
SODIUM: 84 MG	FIBER: 2.4 G	
CARBOHYDRATES: 6.3 G		SUGAR: 3.1 G

GARLIC AND ONIONS KEEP THE DOCTOR AWAY

Vegan, Savory, Paleo

Although it will probably keep more people away than just the doctor, garlic and onion make for an amazing taste combination that will surprise any green-smoothie skeptic. The watercress, celery, and zucchini downplay the intense flavors of the garlic and onion.

24 OUNCES

1 cup watercress

1 celery stalk

1 small green onion, trimmed and chopped

1 small zucchini, peeled and sliced

1 small garlic clove

1¼ cups water, divided

1. Combine watercress, celery, onion, zucchini, garlic, and 1 cup water in the 24-ounce NutriBullet cup and blend until thoroughly combined.

2. Add remaining ¼ cup water and blend until combined.

3. Consume immediately or store with an airtight lid in the refrigerator for no more than 3–4 hours.

PER 24-OUNCE SERVING		
CALORIES: 47	FAT: 0.7 G	PROTEIN: 3.7 G
SODIUM: 72 MG	FIBER: 3.0 G	
CARBOHYDRATES: 9.0 G		SUGAR: 5.7 G

SAVOR THE SODIUM OF CELERY

Vegan, Savory, Paleo

To waken your senses in the early morning or even in the midafternoon, these powerful antioxidant-rich ingredients work together to provide energy, renewed vitality, and overall health. In addition, by consuming celery, the body is more efficient in regulating and maintaining water balance. Celery is rich in vitamins A, C, K, as well as B_6, thiamine, and folic acid. It also provides calcium, potassium, and fiber, and is a natural diuretic.

24 OUNCES

½ cup arugula

½ celery stalk

½ small tomato, sliced

¼ small red bell pepper, top and seeds removed, ribs intact

½ small green onion, trimmed and chopped

½ small garlic clove

1 tablespoons chopped parsley

¾ cups water

1. Combine arugula, celery, tomato, red pepper, onion, garlic, parsley, and water in the 24-ounce NutriBullet cup and blend until thoroughly combined.

2. Consume immediately or store with an airtight lid in the refrigerator for no more than 3–4 hours.

PER 24-OUNCE SERVING		
CALORIES: 26	FAT: 0.2 G	PROTEIN: 1.4 G
SODIUM: 53 MG	FIBER: 2.1 G	
CARBOHYDRATES: 5.5 G		SUGAR: 2.9 G

SPICE IT UP!

Vegan, Savory, Paleo

The arugula, onion, and pepper combine in this recipe for a powerfully delicious treat. Mushrooms are a woody ingredient that tones down the peppery flavor of arugula.

24 OUNCES

1 cup arugula

1 small green onion, trimmed and chopped

½ small red bell pepper, top and seeds removed, ribs intact

½ cup mushrooms, stems intact

1¼ cups water, divided

1. Combine arugula, onion, red pepper, mushrooms, and 1 cup water in the 24-ounce NutriBullet cup and blend until thoroughly combined.

2. Add remaining ¼ cup water and blend until combined.

3. Consume immediately or store with an airtight lid in the refrigerator for no more than 3–4 hours.

PER 24-OUNCE SERVING		
CALORIES: 24	FAT: 0.2 G	PROTEIN: 2.1 G
SODIUM: 18 MG	FIBER: 1.6 G	
CARBOHYDRATES: 4.5 G		SUGAR: 2.8 G

Red Bell Peppers and Vitamins C and A

This beautiful vegetable not only provides a tasty crunch to salads and entrées, but it also provides a whopping dose of both vitamins A and C. One cup of red bell peppers provides over 300 percent of your recommended daily amount of vitamin C and almost 100 percent of your recommended daily amount of vitamin A. This vegetable prevents illnesses like cancer, heart disease, and influenza and protects against free radicals that can cause aged-looking skin, increased fatigue, and zapped energy and mental focus.

PEAR PREVENTION

Sweet

This refreshing smoothie makes a great snack when your body and mind need a lift. The sweet pears, spicy ginger, and rich cabbage and celery combine with the cooling cucumber for an overall refreshing blend.

24 OUNCES

1 cup green cabbage

3 small Bartlett pears, peeled, cored, and sliced

1 small cucumber, peeled and sliced

1 celery stalk

½" knob ginger, peeled

¾ cup kefir, divided

1. Combine cabbage, pears, cucumber, celery, ginger, and ½ cup kefir in the 24-ounce NutriBullet cup and blend until thoroughly combined.

2. Add remaining ¼ cup kefir and blend until combined.

3. Consume immediately or store with an airtight lid in the refrigerator for no more than 3–4 hours.

PER 24-OUNCE SERVING		
CALORIES: 448	FAT: 6.2 G	PROTEIN: 9.9 G
SODIUM: 144 MG	FIBER: 19.8 G	
CARBOHYDRATES: 88.3 G		SUGAR: 55.9 G

HEALTH'S NO JOKE WITH ARTICHOKES

Vegan, Savory, Paleo

The savory ingredients in this green smoothie will take your taste buds over the top. Here you'll find all the nutrients that you need to stay healthy—and satisfied—for any meal!

24 OUNCES

1 cup spinach

4 small artichoke hearts

1 small green onion, trimmed and chopped

2 celery stalks

1¼ cups water, divided

1. Combine spinach, artichokes, onion, celery, and 1 cup water in the 24-ounce NutriBullet cup and blend until thoroughly combined.

2. Add remaining ¼ cup water and blend until combined.

PER 24-OUNCE SERVING		
CALORIES: 95	FAT: 2.6 G	PROTEIN: 5.1 G
SODIUM: 462 MG	FIBER: 8.1 G	
CARBOHYDRATES: 15.8 G		SUGAR: 2.5 G

TURNIP TURNAROUND

Vegan, Savory, Paleo

Turnips are most often seen roasted with other root vegetables around the holidays, but most would never think to include them in a green smoothie. The turnip and carrots make for a delicious taste combination.

24 OUNCES

1 cup watercress

2 small turnips, peeled and chopped

3 small carrots, peeled, sliced, and tops removed

2 celery stalks

1¼ cups water, divided

1. Combine watercress, turnips, carrots, celery, and 1 cup water in the 24-ounce NutriBullet cup and blend until thoroughly combined.

2. Add remaining ¼ cup water and blend until combined.

3. Consume immediately or store with an airtight lid in the refrigerator for no more than 3–4 hours.

PER 24-OUNCE SERVING		
CALORIES: 110	FAT: 0.4 G	PROTEIN: 3.8 G
SODIUM: 272 MG	FIBER: 7.9 G	
CARBOHYDRATES: 25.0 G		SUGAR: 12.9 G

THE POLLINATOR SMOOTHIE

Sweet, Paleo

Suffering from asthma or allergies? Pick up some bee pollen from a local farmers' market or beekeeper. Bee pollen is a wild powder collected by bees from plants and flowers. Granules from this powder are formed as they are accumulated on the bee until it takes it back to the hive and starts all over. Local pollen is preferable because it is collected from the very things in your area that may be aggravating your allergies. Ingesting the pollen works under the same premise as receiving an immunization. It slowly introduces your body to the irritant so that it can build up antibodies to ward off a future infection or irritation.

24 OUNCES

2 cups mixed greens

3 small Bartlett pears, peeled, cored, and sliced

1 tablespoon local bee pollen

2 teaspoons raw honey (local is best)

1¼ cups cooled green tea

1. Combine greens, pears, pollen, honey, and tea in the 24-ounce NutriBullet cup and blend until thoroughly combined.

2. Consume immediately or store with an airtight lid in the refrigerator for no more than 3–4 hours.

PER 24-OUNCE SERVING		
CALORIES: 397	FAT: 1.0 G	PROTEIN: 6.8 G
SODIUM: 75 MG	FIBER: 18.7 G	
CARBOHYDRATES: 90.0 G		SUGAR: 58.5 G

GO, GO, GARLIC!

Vegan, Savory, Paleo

Rich in vitamins and minerals and delivering a wide variety of health benefits, garlic is a powerful addition to any diet in need of a boost. It poses a deterrent to illness and disease and aids in the optimal functioning of the body's natural processes.

24 OUNCES

3 small garlic cloves

1 cup romaine lettuce

2 small tomatoes, sliced

½ cup basil leaves

¼ cup water

1. Crush garlic cloves and let them sit for 1 hour.

2. Combine romaine, tomatoes, basil, water, and garlic in the 24-ounce NutriBullet cup and blend thoroughly until garlic is emulsified.

3. Consume immediately or store with an airtight lid in the refrigerator for no more than 3–4 hours.

PER 24-OUNCE SERVING		
CALORIES: 54	FAT: 0.4 G	PROTEIN: 3.1 G
SODIUM: 13 MG	FIBER: 3.6 G	
CARBOHYDRATES: 11.9 G		SUGAR: 5.5 G

Garlic at Room Temperature

The amazing cancer-fighting benefits and strong antiviral and antibacterial properties in garlic are maximized when the garlic clove has been crushed and allowed to set at room temperature. Heating garlic cloves inhibits the full ability of important enzymes to do their work. Maximize garlic's full potential by preparing it at room temperature in your green smoothies.

BANANA NUT BLEND

Vegan, Sweet

When you think of antioxidant-rich foods, walnuts probably aren't your first thought, but just ¼ cup of walnuts carries almost 100 percent of your daily value of omega-3 fatty acids and is loaded with monounsaturated fats. Of the tree nuts, walnuts, chestnuts, and pecans carry the highest amount of antioxidants, which can prevent illness and reverse oxidative damage done by free radicals.

24 OUNCES

¼ cup walnuts

¾ cup vanilla almond milk, divided

1 cup romaine lettuce

2 small bananas, peeled and sliced

1. Combine walnuts and ½ cup almond milk in the 24-ounce NutriBullet cup and blend until walnuts are completely emulsified.

2. Add romaine, bananas, and remaining ¼ cup almond milk and blend until combined.

3. Consume immediately or store with an airtight lid in the refrigerator for no more than 3–4 hours.

PER 24-OUNCE SERVING		
CALORIES: 54	FAT: 0.4 G	PROTEIN: 3.1 G
SODIUM: 13 MG	FIBER: 3.6 G	
CARBOHYDRATES: 11.9 G		SUGAR: 5.5 G

VEGGIE VARIETY

Vegan, Savory, Paleo

With more variety comes a more beneficial array of the important vitamins and nutrients that keep your body running like an efficient machine.

24 OUNCES

1 cup spinach

1 small tomato, sliced

1 small cucumber, peeled and sliced

2 celery stalks

1 small garlic clove

¾ cup water, divided

1. Combine spinach, tomato, cucumber, celery, garlic, and ½ cup water in the 24-ounce NutriBullet cup and blend until thoroughly combined.

2. Add remaining ¼ cup water and blend until combined.

3. Consume immediately or store with an airtight lid in the refrigerator for no more than 3–4 hours.

PER 24-OUNCE SERVING		
CALORIES: 56	FAT: 0.3 G	PROTEIN: 3.3 G
SODIUM: 101 MG	FIBER: 4.2 G	
CARBOHYDRATES: 11.4 G		SUGAR: 5.8 G

Cucumbers

Cucumbers are available year-round. Store them unwashed in your refrigerator for up to 10 days. Wash them just before using. Leftover cucumbers can be refrigerated again; just tightly wrap them in plastic and they will keep for up to 5 days.

FANTASTIC FENNEL

Vegan, Savory, Paleo

Although it can be found in almost every grocery store's produce section, people rarely purchase or prepare fennel at home. The vitamins and minerals in this veggie make it a must-have, and the taste is amazingly unique. Research shows that many antioxidants interact with and protect each other. Vitamin C, for instance, can react with a damaged vitamin E molecule and convert it back to its antioxidant form, while the antioxidant glutathione can return vitamin C to its original form. Studies also show that vitamin C enhances the protective effects of vitamin E.

24 OUNCES

1 cup romaine lettuce

2 small fennel bulbs

1 small cucumber, peeled and sliced

1 small carrot, peeled, sliced, and top removed

1 celery stalk

1½ cups water, divided

1. Combine romaine, fennel, cucumber, carrot, celery, and 1 cup water in the 24-ounce NutriBullet cup and blend until thoroughly combined.

2. Add remaining ½ cup water and blend until combined.

3. Consume immediately or store with an airtight lid in the refrigerator for no more than 3–4 hours.

PER 24-OUNCE SERVING		
CALORIES: 175	FAT: 1.5 G	PROTEIN: 7.2 G
SODIUM: 294 MG	FIBER: 16.5 G	
CARBOHYDRATES: 40.1 G		SUGAR: 21.4 G

SWEET AND SAVORY BEET

Vegan, Sweet, Paleo

Beets and their greens are filled with antioxidants and vitamins. Paired with the flavorful carrots and cucumbers in this smoothie, they create a sweet and delicious smoothie you're sure to enjoy!

24 OUNCES

1 cup beet greens

2 small beets, sliced

2 small carrots, peeled, sliced, and tops removed

1 small cucumber, peeled and sliced

1¼ cups water, divided

1. Combine beet greens, beets, carrots, cucumber, and 1 cup water in the 24-ounce NutriBullet cup and blend until thoroughly combined.

2. Add remaining ¼ cup water and blend until combined.

3. Consume immediately or store with an airtight lid in the refrigerator for no more than 3–4 hours.

PER 24–OUNCE SERVING		
CALORIES: 137	FAT: 0.4 G	PROTEIN: 5.3 G
SODIUM: 295 MG	FIBER: 9.9 G	
CARBOHYDRATES: 30.3 G		SUGAR: 18.2 G

Vegan, Sweet, Paleo

Vitamin C and a wide variety of other vitamins, minerals, fiber, antioxidants, and amazing flavor in this smoothie create a delicious way to combat illnesses in the tastiest way possible!

24 OUNCES

1 cup watercress

1 small grapefruit, peeled and seeds removed

2 small oranges, peeled and seeds removed

1 small banana, peeled and sliced

¾ cup water, divided

1. Combine watercress, grapefruit, oranges, banana, and ½ cup water in the 24-ounce NutriBullet cup and blend until thoroughly combined.

2. Add remaining ¼ cup water and blend until combined.

3. Consume immediately or store with an airtight lid in the refrigerator for no more than 3–4 hours.

PER 24-OUNCE SERVING		
CALORIES: 310	FAT: 0.5 G	PROTEIN: 6.2 G
SODIUM: 21 MG	FIBER: 11.8 G	
CARBOHYDRATES: 78.4 G		SUGAR: 58.3 G

GREAT GRAPE

Vegan, Sweet, Paleo

Although many people choose grapes as a snack because they're a light, low-calorie, and sweet treat, the health benefits of grapes are another great reason to include them in your daily diet. Containing high levels of manganese, B vitamins, and vitamin C, these fruits also contain powerful polyphenols that can serve as strong antioxidants to help reduce chances of heart disease and fight multiple types of cancer!

24 OUNCES

1 cup watercress

3 cups green seedless grapes

2 small Bartlett pears, peeled, cored, and sliced

¾ cup unsweetened almond milk

1 cup ice

1. Combine watercress, grapes, pears, and almond milk in the 24-ounce NutriBullet cup and blend until thoroughly combined.

2. Add ice and blend until combined.

3. Consume immediately or store with an airtight lid in the refrigerator for no more than 3–4 hours.

PER 24-OUNCE SERVING		
CALORIES: 137	FAT: 0.4 G	PROTEIN: 5.3 G
SODIUM: 295 MG	FIBER: 9.9 G	
CARBOHYDRATES: 30.3 G		SUGAR: 18.2 G

CHAPTER 11

SMOOTHIES FOR PREGNANCY AND WOMEN'S HEALTH

The female body requires different nutrients at different times for various functions, and there's nothing better than sweet treats that also help a woman's brain and body—and those of a baby-to-be—become healthier. The smoothies found in this chapter, like the Nausea No More Smoothie, Fertility Booster Smoothie, and the Berry Bump Smoothie, are dedicated to maximizing the health benefits to the female body through nutrient-dense superfoods that taste great and provide the body with everything it wants and needs. Every recipe is both nutritious and good-tasting to the last drop!

FABULOUS FERTILITY

Vegan, Sweet, Paleo

Whole health from the inside out is the best place to start when you're trying to conceive. Consuming a diet of fruits and vegetables enables your body to function at optimal efficiency. Start by including bright produce in your daily diet. By providing your body with vibrant nutrition following conception, you're providing your baby with the best chance of survival, health, and immunity.

24 OUNCES

1 cup watercress

2 cups cubed and seeded watermelon

½ small cantaloupe, peeled and seeds removed

½" knob ginger, peeled

¾ cup cooled red raspberry tea, divided

1. Combine watercress, watermelon, cantaloupe, ginger, and ½ cup tea in the 24-ounce NutriBullet cup and blend until thoroughly combined.

2. Add remaining ¼ cup tea and blend until combined.

3. Consume immediately or store with an airtight lid in the refrigerator for no more than 3–4 hours.

PER 24-OUNCE SERVING		
CALORIES: 132	FAT: 0.5 G	PROTEIN: 3.6 G
SODIUM: 34 MG	FIBER: 2.4 G	
CARBOHYDRATES: 32.9 G		SUGAR: 27.6 G

APPLE-GINGER DELIGHT

Sweet

The smooth and creamy Greek-style yogurt combines with the apples and ginger in this recipe to yield a truly delicious treat. Enjoy!

24 OUNCES

1 cup romaine lettuce

2 small apples, peeled, cored, and sliced

½" knob ginger, peeled

½ cup Greek-style yogurt, divided

1. Combine romaine, apples, ginger, and ¼ cup yogurt in the 24-ounce NutriBullet cup and blend until thoroughly combined.

2. Add remaining ¼ cup yogurt and blend until combined.

3. Consume immediately or store with an airtight lid in the refrigerator for no more than 3–4 hours.

PER 24-OUNCE SERVING		
CALORIES: 241	FAT: 6.0 G	PROTEIN: 11.6 G
SODIUM: 43 MG	FIBER: 4.4 G	
CARBOHYDRATES: 40.0 G		SUGAR: 31.8 G

Cravings for Sweets

Everybody is familiar with the common cravings. Cravings may vary from person to person—you may crave salty or sweet, for example. Either way, apples have been known to curb most cravings, and also create a feeling of fullness. When a craving hits, eat an apple with a full glass of water and wait 30 minutes. Chances are, your craving will have subsided and you will have replaced a higher-calorie option with a nutritious snack!

NAUSEA NO MORE SMOOTHIE

Vegan, Sweet, Paleo

Anyone who has been pregnant is perplexed by the term "morning sickness," as you know that this disturbance can hit at any time of the day. Bananas are not only a creamy and soothing food that is easy on the stomach, but they contain potassium and B vitamins to keep your body nourished.

24 OUNCES

2 cups Bibb or Boston lettuce

2 small frozen bananas, peeled and sliced

½ cup frozen blueberries

2 cups unsweetened almond milk

1. Combine lettuce, bananas, blueberries, and almond milk in the 24-ounce NutriBullet cup and blend until thoroughly combined.

2. Consume immediately or store with an airtight lid in the refrigerator for no more than 3–4 hours.

PER 24-OUNCE SERVING		
CALORIES: 292	FAT: 5.9 G	PROTEIN: 6.0 G
SODIUM: 327 MG	FIBER: 8.6 G	
CARBOHYDRATES: 58.0 G		SUGAR: 32.3 G

MANGO MATERNITY SMOOTHIE

Vegan, Sweet, Paleo

In addition to being velvety and soothing, this exotic smoothie is high in folate due to the spinach and mango. Folate is required in a woman's diet to help prevent birth defects. This is a great prenatal drink to add to your diet as folate is especially necessary before conception and during the first months of pregnancy.

24 OUNCES

2 cups spinach

2 cups frozen mango cubes

½ cup frozen pineapple cubes

2 cups unsweetened CoconutMilk

1. Combine spinach, mango, pineapple, and CoconutMilk in the 24-ounce NutriBullet cup and blend until thoroughly combined.

2. Consume immediately or store with an airtight lid in the refrigerator for no more than 3–4 hours.

PER 24-OUNCE SERVING		
CALORIES: 389	FAT: 8.1 G	PROTEIN: 2.4 G
SODIUM: 117 MG	FIBER: 8.0 G	
CARBOHYDRATES: 78.2 G		SUGAR: 58.3 G

CRANBABY SMOOTHIE

Vegan, Sweet, Paleo

Women are susceptible to urinary tract infections (UTIs) during pregnancy. Cranberries can be very helpful as a preventative during this time as it is believed that the antioxidants present in them can prevent certain bacteria from sticking to the walls of the urinary tract and causing an infection.

24 OUNCES

2 cups kale

1 cup cranberries

1 cup frozen mixed berries

2 cups unsweetened almond milk

1 teaspoon pure maple syrup

1. Combine kale, cranberries, mixed berries, almond milk, and maple syrup in the 24-ounce NutriBullet cup and blend until thoroughly combined.

2. Consume immediately or store with an airtight lid in the refrigerator for no more than 3–4 hours.

PER 24-OUNCE SERVING		
CALORIES: 213	FAT: 5.6 G	PROTEIN: 4.8 G
SODIUM: 334 MG	FIBER: 10.7 G	
CARBOHYDRATES: 38.1 G		SUGAR: 20.7 G

TUMMY LOVE SMOOTHIE

Vegan, Sweet, Paleo

Ginger has long been used for nausea and morning sickness. Just be careful: It can also cause heartburn in some mommies. A knob of ginger can be difficult to peel because of the grooves and bumps. Instead, use a spoon's edge to scrape away the skin. It's much easier than trying to use a vegetable peeler . . . your fingertips will thank you.

24 OUNCES

2 cups spinach

2 small apples of choice, peeled, cored, and sliced

2 small carrots, peeled, sliced, and tops removed

½" knob ginger, peeled

¼ teaspoon cinnamon

1¾ cups unsweetened almond milk

1. Combine spinach, apples, carrots, ginger, cinnamon, and almond milk in the 24-ounce NutriBullet cup and blend until thoroughly combined.

2. Consume immediately or store with an airtight lid in the refrigerator for no more than 3–4 hours.

PER 24-OUNCE SERVING		
CALORIES: 233	FAT: 4.8 G	PROTEIN: 5.2 G
SODIUM: 396 MG	FIBER: 7.9 G	
CARBOHYDRATES: 46.2 G		SUGAR: 31.7 G

CANKLES BE GONE SMOOTHIE

Vegan, Sweet, Paleo

Swollen ankles are common during pregnancy due to water retention. Give yourself a break from standing. While soaking your swollen feet in a warm Epsom salts bath (the miracle cure for sore muscles), sip this smoothie full of potassium and antioxidants known for reducing swelling.

24 OUNCES

2 cups spinach

1 cup peeled and seeded cantaloupe

1 small orange, peeled and seeds removed

1 small carrot, peeled, sliced, and top removed

1¾ cups coconut water

1. Combine spinach, cantaloupe, orange, carrot, and coconut water in the 24-ounce NutriBullet cup and blend until thoroughly combined.

2. Consume immediately or store with an airtight lid in the refrigerator for no more than 3–4 hours.

PER 24-OUNCE SERVING		
CALORIES: 209	FAT: 0.5 G	PROTEIN: 5.4 G
SODIUM: 217 MG	FIBER: 6.5 G	
CARBOHYDRATES: 49.5 G		SUGAR: 41.0 G

BUNDLE OF C SMOOTHIE

Vegan, Sweet, Paleo

This refreshing smoothie is bursting with vitamin C. The natural nutrients in oranges, strawberries, and sweet peppers are necessary for the formation of collagen, which works naturally to help form the cartilage, tendons, bones, and skin of your growing bundle of joy.

24 OUNCES

2 cups spinach

1 small orange, peeled and seeds removed

1 cup strawberries, tops removed

1/2 small red bell pepper, top and seeds removed, ribs intact

1¾ cups coconut water

1. Combine spinach, orange, strawberries, pepper, and coconut water in the 24-ounce NutriBullet cup and blend until thoroughly combined.

2. Consume immediately or store with an airtight lid in the refrigerator for no more than 3–4 hours.

PER 24-OUNCE SERVING		
CALORIES: 192	FAT: 0.5 G	PROTEIN: 4.9 G
SODIUM: 160 MG	FIBER: 7.3 G	
CARBOHYDRATES: 44.9 G		SUGAR: 34.6 G

LI'L PUMPKIN SMOOTHIE

Vegan, Sweet, Paleo

Take care of your growing li'l pumpkin with this soothing blend of pumpkin and spices. When pregnant, your hips, back, and abdomen start to stretch and loosen in preparation for the birth. The protein in pumpkin seeds will help repair and prepare your muscles. For a snack, drizzle the seeds with a little avocado oil and bake them until crispy. Let cool and enjoy.

24 OUNCES

2 cups mixed greens

½ cup pumpkin purée

1 small frozen banana, peeled and sliced

2 tablespoons pumpkin seeds

½ teaspoon pumpkin pie spice

1¾ cups unsweetened almond milk

1. Combine greens, pumpkin purée, banana, pumpkin seeds, pumpkin pie spice, and almond milk in the 24-ounce NutriBullet cup and blend until thoroughly combined.

2. Consume immediately or store with an airtight lid in the refrigerator for no more than 3–4 hours.

PER 24–OUNCE SERVING		
CALORIES: 247	FAT: 11.4 G	PROTEIN: 9.3 G
SODIUM: 350 MG	FIBER: 7.2 G	
CARBOHYDRATES: 33.3 G		SUGAR: 14.6 G

BERRY BUMP SMOOTHIE

Vegan, Sweet, Paleo

When mama's happy, everyone's happy! Satisfying and refreshing ingredients combine in this flavorful smoothie that's packed with a large number of minerals and vitamins required for prenatal support and development. Constipation is a common occurrence during pregnancy; the goji berries in this smoothie work as a natural laxative.

24 OUNCES

2 cups romaine lettuce

¼ cup fresh goji berries

¼ cup frozen blueberries

1 small kiwi, peeled

1 celery stalk

1 small apple, peeled, cored, and sliced

1¾ cups coconut water

1. Combine romaine, goji berries, blueberries, kiwi, celery, apple, and coconut water in the 24-ounce NutriBullet cup and blend until thoroughly combined.

2. Consume immediately or store with an airtight lid in the refrigerator for no more than 3–4 hours.

PER 24-OUNCE SERVING		
CALORIES: 315	FAT: 0.8 G	PROTEIN: 7.5 G
SODIUM: 195 MG	FIBER: 19.0 G	
CARBOHYDRATES: 77.9 G		SUGAR: 45.3 G

HOT MAMA SMOOTHIE

Vegan, Savory, Paleo

Spicy foods are perfectly safe to eat when you're pregnant. With that said, they're a personal preference because heartburn is a common ailment during pregnancy. Spicy foods can aggravate this heartburn, especially in the third trimester when the baby is larger, causing stomach acid to be pushed up to the esophagus. But if that doesn't bother you, try this delicious and spicy smoothie.

24 OUNCES

2 cups arugula

1 small jalapeño, seeds removed

2 small apples, peeled, cored, and sliced

1 small orange, peeled and seeds removed

½" knob ginger, peeled

1¾ cups water

1. Combine arugula, jalapeño, apples, orange, ginger, and water in the 24-ounce NutriBullet cup and blend until thoroughly combined.

2. Consume immediately or store with an airtight lid in the refrigerator for no more than 3–4 hours.

PER 24-OUNCE SERVING		
CALORIES: 185	FAT: 0.4 G	PROTEIN: 2.8 G
SODIUM: 26 MG	FIBER: 6.8 G	
CARBOHYDRATES: 47.5 G		SUGAR: 37.1 G

Sweet, Paleo

If you are trying to get pregnant, you can start preparing your body for this ultra-important journey. Goodbye to inflammation-causing processed yuck and junk foods. Hello to protein, healthy carbohydrates, good fats, folate, iron, magnesium, and all the other vitamins and nutrients needed to grow a healthy little human.

24 OUNCES

2 cups baby spinach

6 small figs

½ small frozen banana, peeled and sliced

¼ cup unsweetened coconut flakes

½" knob ginger, peeled

2 teaspoons raw honey

1¾ cups coconut water

1. Combine spinach, figs, banana, coconut flakes, ginger, honey, and coconut water in the 24-ounce NutriBullet cup and blend until thoroughly combined.

2. Consume immediately or store with an airtight lid in the refrigerator for no more than 3–4 hours.

PER 24-OUNCE SERVING		
CALORIES: 453	FAT: 10.9 G	PROTEIN: 6.1 G
SODIUM: 165 MG	FIBER: 11.6 G	
CARBOHYDRATES: 93.4 G		SUGAR: 74.6 G

STORK ALERT SMOOTHIE

Sweet, Paleo

Many people believe that women who consume a lot of fruits and vegetables (but no bananas) will have a girl because of the magnesium and calcium. Boys are, of course, made from potassium. So add this to your bag of old wives' tales. This smoothie has a little of everything, so maybe you'll have twins—a boy and a girl!

24 OUNCES

2 cups kale

1 small banana, peeled and sliced

1 small carrot, peeled, sliced, and top removed

3 small plums, peeled and pitted

1 tablespoon sunflower seeds

2 teaspoons raw honey

1¾ cups coconut water

1. Combine kale, banana, carrot, plums, sunflower seeds, honey, and coconut water in the 24-ounce NutriBullet cup and blend until thoroughly combined.

2. Consume immediately or store with an airtight lid in the refrigerator for no more than 3–4 hours.

PER 24-OUNCE SERVING		
CALORIES: 374	FAT: 4.6 G	PROTEIN: 6.8 G
SODIUM: 158 MG	FIBER: 8.7 G	
CARBOHYDRATES: 83.2 G		SUGAR: 62.1 G

FOLATE FOR FINE SPINES SMOOTHIE

Sweet, Paleo

Among the important vitamins and minerals found to prevent birth defects, one of the most well-known is folate. Studies have shown that proper levels of folate in pregnancy reduce or remedy the chance of neural and spinal-tube defects. You can take a prenatal vitamin that includes folate, but what about natural sources? Eating a diet rich in deep-green leafy veggies can provide a great amount of folate naturally.

24 OUNCES

1½ cups spinach

½ cup broccoli spears

1 cup frozen pineapple cubes

2 teaspoons raw honey

1¾ cups unsweetened CoconutMilk

1. Combine spinach, broccoli, pineapple, honey, and CoconutMilk in the 24-ounce NutriBullet cup and blend until thoroughly combined.

2. Consume immediately or store with an airtight lid in the refrigerator for no more than 3–4 hours.

PER 24-OUNCE SERVING		
CALORIES: 229	FAT: 7.1 G	PROTEIN: 2.9 G
SODIUM: 80 MG	FIBER: 4.0 G	
CARBOHYDRATES: 38.6 G		SUGAR: 16.1 G

PREGNANT BRAIN SMOOTHIE

Vegan, Sweet, Paleo

Not only is vitamin C an important addition to your diet for its strong immunity-building power; this vitamin also benefits the expectant mom by providing optimal brain functioning. That means better mental clarity, improved focus, and an overall feeling of awareness instead of the mental fuzziness commonly referred to as "pregnant brain."

24 OUNCES

2 cups watercress

2 small tangerines, peeled and seeds removed

½ small grapefruit, peeled and seeds removed

½ cup frozen pineapple cubes

½ cup peeled and seeded cantaloupe

1¾ cups cooled red raspberry tea

1. Combine watercress, tangerines, grapefruit, pineapple, cantaloupe, and tea in the 24-ounce NutriBullet cup and blend until thoroughly combined.

2. Consume immediately or store with an airtight lid in the refrigerator for no more than 3–4 hours.

PER 24-OUNCE SERVING		
CALORIES: 228	FAT: 0.5 G	PROTEIN: 5.4 G
SODIUM: 46 MG	FIBER: 7.3 G	
CARBOHYDRATES: 56.7 G		SUGAR: 38.5 G

APPENDIX A
U.S./METRIC CONVERSION CHART

VOLUME CONVERSIONS

U.S. Volume Measure	Metric Equivalent
⅛ teaspoon	0.5 milliliter
¼ teaspoon	1 milliliter
½ teaspoon	2 milliliters
1 teaspoon	5 milliliters
½ tablespoon	7 milliliters
1 tablespoon (3 teaspoons)	15 milliliters
2 tablespoons (1 fluid ounce)	30 milliliters
¼ cup (4 tablespoons)	60 milliliters
⅓ cup	90 milliliters
½ cup (4 fluid ounces)	125 milliliters
⅔ cup	160 milliliters
¾ cup (6 fluid ounces)	180 milliliters
1 cup (16 tablespoons)	250 milliliters
1 pint (2 cups)	500 milliliters
1 quart (4 cups)	1 liter (about)

WEIGHT CONVERSIONS

U.S. Weight Measure	Metric Equivalent
½ ounce	15 grams
1 ounce	30 grams
2 ounces	60 grams
3 ounces	85 grams
¼ pound (4 ounces)	115 grams
½ pound (8 ounces)	225 grams
¾ pound (12 ounces)	340 grams
1 pound (16 ounces)	454 grams

LENGTH CONVERSIONS

U.S. Length Measure	Metric Equivalent
¼ inch	0.6 centimeters
½ inch	1.2 centimeters
¾ inch	1.9 centimeters
1 inch	2.5 centimeters
1½ inches	3.8 centimeters
1 foot	0.3 meters
1 yard	0.9 meters

OVEN TEMPERATURE CONVERSIONS

Degrees Fahrenheit	Degrees Celsius
200 degrees F	95 degrees C
250 degrees F	120 degrees C
275 degrees F	135 degrees C
300 degrees F	150 degrees C
325 degrees F	160 degrees C
350 degrees F	180 degrees C
375 degrees F	190 degrees C
400 degrees F	205 degrees C
425 degrees F	220 degrees C
450 degrees F	230 degrees C

BAKING PAN SIZES

American	Metric
8 x 1½ inch round baking pan	20 x 4 cm cake tin
9 x 1½ inch round baking pan	23 x 3.5 cm cake tin
11 x 7 x 1½ inch baking pan	28 x 18 x 4 cm baking tin
13 x 9 x 2 inch baking pan	30 x 20 x 5 cm baking tin
2 quart rectangular baking dish	30 x 20 x 3 cm baking tin
15 x 10 x 2 inch baking pan	30 x 25 x 2 cm baking tin (Swiss roll tin)
9 inch pie plate	22 x 4 or 23 x 4 cm pie plate
7 or 8 inch springform pan	18 or 20 cm springform or loose bottom cake tin
9 x 5 x 3 inch loaf pan	23 x 13 x 7 cm or 2 lb narrow loaf or pate tin
1½ quart casserole	1.5 liter casserole
2 quart casserole	2 liter casserole

SMOOTHIES BY TYPE

PALEO

A Biker's Best Friend
A Fruity Flush
A Glad Gallbladder
A Grape Way to Bone Health
A Peppery Way to Promote Health
A Spicy Blue Blast
Ache Aid
Agent Pineapple Against Arthritis
Ahhh, Sweet Greens!
Alcohol Recovery Recipe
Amazing Apples for Digestion
An Apple Pie Day
Antioxidant Assist
Apple Broccoli Detox Blend
Apple Celery for Hydration
Apple Peach
Apple Pie for Weight Loss
Asparagus Carrot
Backwards Berry
Beany Spinach
Beet the Bloat
Berries for Health
Berry Bump Smoothie
Berry Pretty Smoothie
Bone Up with Blackberries
Breathe Easy Smoothie
Bright Fight Against Disease
Broccoli Blastoff
Broccoli Detox
Bundle of C Smoothie
Cabbage Calms Indigestion
Cacao Craziness
Calming Cucumber
Cankles Be Gone Smoothie
Cantaloupe Creation
Cantaloupe for Cancer Prevention

Cantaloupe Quencher
Carotenes Against Cancer
Carrot Cleanser
Carrot Commando
Carrot Top of the Morning to You
Cauliflower to the Rescue
Cherry Vanilla Respiratory Relief
Chocolatey Dream
Cinch Pounds with Citrus
Citrus Berry Blast
Cleanse Your Body with Sweet
  Citrus
Cleansing Broccoli Smoothie
Cleansing Cranberry
Cocoa Strong Smoothie
Collide with Collards
Colorful Cleansing Combo
Colorful Combo for Cancer Prevention
Colors of Success
Cool Off Colitis
Cranbaby Smoothie
Cucumber Cooler
Cucumber Zing
Double-Duty Delight
Dreamy Digestion
Energetic Artichoke Smoothie
Fabulous Fertility
Fabulous Fructose
Fantastic Fennel
Fat-Burning Fuel
Fennel-Cucumber Smoothie
Fertility Booster Smoothie
Fiber Flush Smoothie
Flush Out Fat with Fiber
Folate for Fine Spines Smoothie
Fruity Fresh Immunity Blast
Garlic and Onions Keep the Doctor

Away
Garlic Gets the Pounds Off
Garlic Zucchini Cleanse
Gear Up with Garlic
Get Rid of Gas!
Ginger Ale Smoothie
Ginger and Apple Cleansing Blend
Ginger and Spice Make Everything
  Nice
Ginger Apple
Ginger Green Tea Smoothie
Go, Go, Garlic!
Gorgeous Greens for a Gorgeous
  Body
Grapefruit and Cucumber Energy
GrAppleBerry
Great Grape
Green Citrus
Green Clean Smoothie
Green Garlic Smoothie
Green Sweet Citrus
Green Tea Carrot Smoothie
Green Tea Metabolism Booster
Health's No Joke with Artichokes
Heartburn, Be Gone
Herbal Peach
Hot Mama Smoothie
Illness Preventer
Indigestion Inhibitor
Kale and Carrot Flush
Keep It Moving
Killer Kale Kickoff
Li'l Pumpkin Smoothie
Liven Up the Liver
Luscious Lemon
Manage Your Weight with Mangos
Mango Berry
Mango Digestion Smoothie
Mango Maternity Smoothie
Mango Tango
Mega Magnesium
Memory Maintainer
Mental Makeover

Metabolism Max Out
Minty Mango Metabolism Maxi-
  mizer
Move Over, Motion Sickness!
Nausea No More Smoothie
Oh My! Omegas
Orange You Glad You Got Up for
  This?
Papaya Berry Blend
"Pea" Is for Prevention
Pear Splendor
Pears with a Tart Twist
Pears, Apples, and Ginger
Peas, Please!
Perfect Pears and Pineapples
Pineapple-Papaya Protection
Pleasantly Pear
Pomegranate Preventer
Popeye's Favorite
Powerful Parsnips
Pregnant Brain Smoothie
Red Bells Make Hearts Ring
Red Pepper Relief
Refresh That Body
Refreshing Reprieve
Romaine to the Rescue!
Root Veggie Variety
Savor Cancer Prevention
Savor the Sodium of Celery
Savory Slim Down
Slim Down with This Sweet Treat
Smart Start
Smooth Carrot Apple
Smooth Citrus for Smooth Diges-
  tion
Spice It Up!
Spicy Refreshment
Spicy Stomach Soother
Spinach-y Sweet Smoothie
Splendid Citrus
Splendid Melon
Stork Alert Smoothie
Sunburn Soother

Super Celery Smoothie
Sweet and Savory Beet
Sweet Fiber
Sweet Ginger Melon
Sweet Potato Smoothie
Sweet Spinach Spinner
The Bright Bloat Beater
The Constipation Cure
The Deep Colors of Detox
The Pollinator Smoothie
The Slump Bumper
The Spicy Savior
Tomatillo Mary Smoothie
Trail Mix Smoothie
Tummy Love Smoothie
Tummy Protector
Turnip Turnaround
Veggie Variety
Very Green Smoothie
Very Important Vitamin C
Vitamin C Cancer Prevention
Vivacious Vitamin C
Watercress Berry
What the Hill Smoothie
Zap Pounds with Zippy Zucchini
Zoom with Zucchini

SAVORY

A Glad Gallbladder
A Peppery Way to Promote Health
Antioxidant Assist
Asparagus Carrot
Beany Spinach
Broccoli Blastoff
Cabbage Calms Indigestion
Calming Cucumber
Collide with Collards
Cool Off Colitis
Fantastic Fennel
Fennel-Cucumber Smoothie
Garlic and Onions Keep the Doctor
  Away
Garlic Gets the Pounds Off

Garlic Zucchini Cleanse
Gear Up with Garlic
Get Rid of Gas!
Ginger and Apple Cleansing Blend
Go, Go, Garlic!
Green Garlic Smoothie
Health's No Joke with Artichokes
Heartburn, Be Gone
Hot Mama Smoothie
Keep It Moving
Killer Kale Kickoff
Luscious Lemon
Mega Magnesium
Memory Maintainer
Mental Makeover
Popeye's Favorite
Rapid Recovery
Red Bells Make Hearts Ring
Red Pepper Relief
Romaine to the Rescue!
Savor Cancer Prevention
Savor the Sodium of Celery
Savory Slim Down
Spice It Up!
Spicy Stomach Soother
Super Celery Smoothie
The Constipation Cure
The Deep Colors of Detox
The Spicy Savior
Tomatillo Mary Smoothie
Tummy Protector
Turnip Turnaround
Veggie Variety
Very Green Smoothie
Zap Pounds with Zippy Zucchini
Zoom with Zucchini

SWEET

A Berry Great Morning
A Biker's Best Friend
A Cool Blend for Blood Sugars
A Fruity Flush
A Grape Way to Bone Health

A Spicy Blue Blast
A Sweet Smoothie for Health
A Sweet Step to Great Health
A Yogi's Favorite
Ache Aid
Agent Pineapple Against Arthritis
Ahhh, Sweet Greens!
Alcohol Recovery Recipe
Amazing Apples for Digestion
An Apple Pie Day
Apple Broccoli Detox Blend
Apple Celery for Hydration
Apple Peach
Apple Pie for Weight Loss
Apple-Ginger Delight
Backwards Berry
Banana Berry Boost
Banana Nut Bread
Beet the Bloat
Berries and Bananas for Bone
  Health
Berries for Health
Berry Bump Smoothie
Berry Pretty Smoothie
Blackberry Watercress Smoothie
Blueberry Burst
Bone Up with Blackberries
Breathe Easy Smoothie
Bright Fight Against Disease
Broccoli Detox
Bundle of C Smoothie
Cacao Craziness
Cankles Be Gone Smoothie
Cantaloupe Creation
Cantaloupe for Cancer Prevention
Cantaloupe Quencher
Carotenes Against Cancer
Carrot Cleanser
Carrot Commando
Carrot Top of the Morning to You
Cauliflower to the Rescue
Cherry Vanilla Respiratory Relief
Chocolatey Dream

Cinch Pounds with Citrus
Citrus Berry Blast
Cleanse Your Body with Sweet
  Citrus
Cleansing Broccoli Smoothie
Cleansing Cranberry
Cocoa Strong Smoothie
Colorful Cleansing Combo
Colorful Combo for Cancer Preven-
  tion
Colors of Success
Cool Cucumber Melon
Cranbaby Smoothie
Cucumber Cooler
Cucumber Zing
Double-Duty Delight
Dreamy Digestion
Energetic Artichoke Smoothie
Fabulous Fertility
Fabulous Fructose
Fat-Burning Fuel
Fertility Booster Smoothie
Fiber Flush Smoothie
Flush Out Fat with Fiber
Folate for Fine Spines Smoothie
Fruity Fresh Immunity Blast
Ginger Ale Smoothie
Ginger and Apple Cleansing Blend
Ginger and Spice Make Everything
  Nice
Ginger Apple
Ginger Green Tea Smoothie
Gorgeous Greens for a Gorgeous
  Body
Grapefruit and Cucumber Energy
GrAppleBerry
Great Grape
Green Citrus
Green Clean Smoothie
Green Sweet Citrus
Green Tea Carrot Smoothie
Green Tea Metabolism Booster
Herbal Peach

Illness Preventer
Indigestion Inhibitor
Kale and Carrot Flush
Li'l Pumpkin Smoothie
Liven Up the Liver
Luscious Lemon-Lime
Manage Your Weight with Mangos
Mango Berry
Mango Digestion Smoothie
Mango Maternity Smoothie
Mango Tango
Metabolism Max Out
Minty Madness
Minty Mango Metabolism Maxi-
  mizer
Move Over, Motion Sickness!
Nausea No More Smoothie
Oh My! Omegas
Orange You Glad You Got Up for
  This?
Papaya Berry Blend
"Pea" Is for Prevention
Pear Prevention
Pear Splendor
Pears with a Tart Twist
Pears, Apples, and Ginger
Peas, Please!
Perfect Pears and Pineapples
Pineapple-Papaya Protection
Pleasantly Pear
Pomegranate Preventer
Powerful Parsnips
Pregnant Brain Smoothie
Protein Packer
Refresh That Body
Refreshing Reprieve
Root Veggie Variety
Runner's Delight
Slim Down with This Sweet Treat
Smart Start
Smooth Carrot Apple
Smooth Citrus for Smooth Diges-
  tion

Spicy Refreshment
Spinach-y Sweet Smoothie
Splendid Citrus
Splendid Melon
Stork Alert Smoothie
Strawberry-Rhubarb Healing
  Smoothie
Sunburn Soother
Sweet and Savory Beet
Sweet Fiber
Sweet Ginger Melon
Sweet Potato Smoothie
Sweet Spinach Spinner
Swimmer's Sensation
The Bright Bloat Beater
The Pollinator Smoothie
The Slump Bumper
Trail Mix Smoothie
Tummy Love Smoothie
Very Important Vitamin C
Vitamin C Cancer Prevention
Vivacious Vitamin C
Wake Up and Smell the Grapefruit
  Smoothie
Watercress Berry
What the Hill Smoothie
Wonder Watermelon

VEGAN

A Berry Great Morning
A Biker's Best Friend
A Fruity Flush
A Glad Gallbladder
A Grape Way to Bone Health
A Peppery Way to Promote Health
A Spicy Blue Blast
Ache Aid
Agent Pineapple Against Arthritis
Ahhh, Sweet Greens!
Alcohol Recovery Recipe
Amazing Apples for Digestion
An Apple Pie Day
Antioxidant Assist

Apple Broccoli Detox Blend
Apple Celery for Hydration
Apple Peach
Apple Pie for Weight Loss
Asparagus Carrot
Backwards Berry
Banana Nut Bread
Beany Spinach
Beet the Bloat
Berries for Health
Berry Bump Smoothie
Berry Pretty Smoothie
Bone Up with Blackberries
Breathe Easy Smoothie
Bright Fight Against Disease
Broccoli Blastoff
Broccoli Detox
Bundle of C Smoothie
Cabbage Calms Indigestion
Cacao Craziness
Calming Cucumber
Cankles Be Gone Smoothie
Cantaloupe Creation
Cantaloupe for Cancer Prevention
Cantaloupe Quencher
Carotenes Against Cancer
Carrot Cleanser
Carrot Commando
Carrot Top of the Morning to You
Cauliflower to the Rescue
Cherry Vanilla Respiratory Relief
Chocolatey Dream
Cinch Pounds with Citrus
Citrus Berry Blast
Cleanse Your Body with Sweet
  Citrus
Cleansing Broccoli Smoothie
Cleansing Cranberry
Cocoa Strong Smoothie
Collide with Collards
Colorful Cleansing Combo
Colorful Combo for Cancer Preven-
  tion

Colors of Success
Cool Off Colitis
Cranbaby Smoothie
Cucumber Cooler
Cucumber Zing
Double-Duty Delight
Dreamy Digestion
Energetic Artichoke Smoothie
Fabulous Fertility
Fabulous Fructose
Fantastic Fennel
Fat-Burning Fuel
Fennel-Cucumber Smoothie
Fiber Flush Smoothie
Flush Out Fat with Fiber
Fruity Fresh Immunity Blast
Garlic and Onions Keep the Doctor
  Away
Garlic Gets the Pounds Off
Garlic Zucchini Cleanse
Gear Up with Garlic
Get Rid of Gas!
Ginger Ale Smoothie
Ginger and Apple Cleansing Blend
Ginger and Spice Make Everything
  Nice
Ginger Apple
Ginger Green Tea Smoothie
Go, Go, Garlic!
Gorgeous Greens for a Gorgeous
  Body
Grapefruit and Cucumber Energy
GrAppleBerry
Great Grape
Green Citrus
Green Clean Smoothie
Green Garlic Smoothie
Green Sweet Citrus
Green Tea Carrot Smoothie
Green Tea Metabolism Booster
Health's No Joke with Artichokes
Heartburn, Be Gone
Herbal Peach

Hot Mama Smoothie
Illness Preventer
Indigestion Inhibitor
Kale and Carrot Flush
Keep It Moving
Killer Kale Kickoff
Li'l Pumpkin Smoothie
Liven Up the Liver
Luscious Lemon
Manage Your Weight with Mangos
Mango Berry
Mango Digestion Smoothie
Mango Maternity Smoothie
Mango Tango
Mega Magnesium
Memory Maintainer
Mental Makeover
Metabolism Max Out
Minty Madness
Minty Mango Metabolism Maximizer
Move Over, Motion Sickness!
Nausea No More Smoothie
Oh My! Omegas
Orange You Glad You Got Up for This?
Papaya Berry Blend
"Pea" Is for Prevention
Pear Splendor
Pears with a Tart Twist
Pears, Apples, and Ginger
Peas, Please!
Perfect Pears and Pineapples
Pineapple-Papaya Protection
Pleasantly Pear
Pomegranate Preventer
Popeye's Favorite
Powerful Parsnips
Pregnant Brain Smoothie
Red Bells Make Hearts Ring
Red Pepper Relief
Refresh That Body
Refreshing Reprieve

Romaine to the Rescue!
Root Veggie Variety
Savor Cancer Prevention
Savor the Sodium of Celery
Savory Slim Down
Slim Down with This Sweet Treat
Smart Start
Smooth Carrot Apple
Smooth Citrus for Smooth Digestion
Spice It Up!
Spicy Refreshment
Spicy Stomach Soother
Spinach-y Sweet Smoothie
Splendid Citrus
Splendid Melon
Sunburn Soother
Super Celery Smoothie
Sweet and Savory Beet
Sweet Fiber
Sweet Ginger Melon
Sweet Potato Smoothie
Sweet Spinach Spinner
The Bright Bloat Beater
The Constipation Cure
The Deep Colors of Detox
The Slump Bumper
The Spicy Savior
Tomatillo Mary Smoothie
Trail Mix Smoothie
Tummy Love Smoothie
Tummy Protector
Turnip Turnaround
Veggie Variety
Very Green Smoothie
Very Important Vitamin C
Vitamin C Cancer Prevention
Vivacious Vitamin C
Watercress Berry
What the Hill Smoothie
Zap Pounds with Zippy Zucchini
Zoom with Zucchini

INDEX